THE LIBRARY OF CONTEMPORARY THOUGHT

*America's most original voices
tackle today's most provocative issues*

SUSAN ISAACS

BRAVE DAMES AND WIMPETTES

What Women Are Really Doing on Page and Screen

"Our media—our journalism, our art—abound with wounded women. We seem to have lost our sturdy immigrant past, forgotten that we once had strong and gallant women heroes like Willa Cather's *My Antonia*. We are descendants of brave dames like these, not a nation of weaklings. . . . A damsel-in-distress, movie-of-the-week mentality has infected our film and fiction. Despite the most recent revolution in women's rights, we are still being portrayed as the gender of the quivering lower lip. . . ."

Also by Susan Isaacs

NOVELS

Compromising Positions

Close Relations

Almost Paradise

Shining Through

Magic Hour

After All These Years

Lily White

Red, White and Blue

SCREENPLAYS

Compromising Positions

Hello Again

Brave Dames
and
Wimpettes

What Women Are Really
Doing on Page and Screen

Susan Isaacs

The Library of Contemporary Thought
The Ballantine Publishing Group • New York

The Library of Contemporary Thought
Published by The Ballantine Publishing Group

http://www.randomhouse.com/BB/

Library of Congress Cataloging-in-Publication Data
Isaacs, Susan.
Brave dames and wimpettes : what women are really doing on
page and screen / Susan Isaacs.—1st ed.
p.   cm.
ISBN 0-345-42281-3 (trade : alk. paper)
1. Women in motion pictures.   2. Women on television.
3. Women in literature.   I. Title.
PN1995.9.W6I82   1999
791.43'652042—dc21   98-47870
                                                              CIP

Text design by Holly Johnson
Cover design by Ruth Ross
Cover photos: photo of Calista Flockhart © Jeff Spicer/
Alpha/Globe Photos, Inc.; *Gone with the Wind* © Selznick/
MGM (courtesy of Kobal Collection)

Manufactured in the United States of America

First Edition: January 1999

10 9 8 7 6 5 4 3 2 1

Once again, to Elkan Abramowitz,
the best person in the world

Acknowledgments

Elizabeth J. Carroll did much of the research for this work, but she did far more than come up with facts. She has a first-rate intellect, a litigator's persistence, and a dry wit; she brought all these qualities to the project. I could not have written *Brave Dames and Wimpettes* without her extraordinary efforts.

This book began with an article I wrote for the *New York Times* Arts and Leisure section, "Sisterhood Isn't So Powerful in the Movies," January 14, 1990. Ever since, I've been thinking about the quality of the women I meet in novels and movies and on TV. Naturally, some of that thought has been shaped by my reading. While I do not agree with every opinion expressed in the following books, I found them all incisive, provocative, and well written:

> *Backlash: The Undeclared War Against*
> *American Women,* by Susan Faludi
> *From Reverence to Rape: The Treatment of*
> *Women in the Movies,* by Molly Haskell
> *The Morning After: Sex, Fear and Feminism,*
> by Katie Roiphe
> *Where the Girls Are: Growing Up Female*
> *with the Mass Media,* by Susan J.
> Douglas

Lastly, I want to thank my family of literary critics and film mavens for their love, encouragement, freely offered advice, and great humor.

1

I Am Woman,
Hear Me Roar . . .

*About How I've Been Abused, Misused,
Violated, and Discriminated Against*

OH, SURE, WE TALK A good game: Assertiveness. Power. Take back the night. Just
do it. After all, we've been through a revolution in
women's rights in the last thirty-odd years. Except
even after all the fireworks, speeches, and marches,
our female icons seem to me a pretty pathetic lot.
Ditto for many of the characters we meet these
days in movies, on TV, and in novels. There are
not enough of those courageous spirits to reflect
the times. I miss the Jane Eyres, my heroes, the
brave dames I always admired and sometimes loved.
Too many of today's female protagonists are still
tremulous, willfully naive, self-absorbed, and self-
pitying, queens of passive aggression. They are the

Madame Bovarys. Wimpettes. And too many of us accept them as feminist heroes.

As no doubt you know, a wimp is someone weak and ineffectual. A wimp is the ninety-eight-pound weakling who gets sand kicked in his face by the pumped-up bully not merely because he is a physical lightweight, but because he is a moral one as well. Instead of trying to reason with the bully, or venturing a sock in the snoot, the wimp says, in essence: Do with me what you will.

A wimpette—a word I made up because I needed it—is a woman who is weak or ineffectual because *she gives in, without a real fight, to the limits imposed on her by virtue of her gender.* A wimpette deserves the diminutive at the end of her name. Her "no" rarely has an exclamation point. Her voice used to be pitched high—either nauseatingly perky or breathy—as if to underscore her utter lack of testosterone. She sounded like Minnie Mouse or Marilyn Monroe. Now she may simply be mute, like Holly Hunter as Ada in *The Piano*. Or she may in fact talk the talk, but she lacks the guts to walk the walk: A wimpette may tell us, with words or grimaces, "Ooh, ooh, I'm trying so hard!" yet she never quite manages to rise above her own fragility, be it psychic or somatic—unless she is helped by a man. At her worst the wimpette puts the blame for her failures on society, on men, on

her mother. At her best she is feisty or spunky—
never strong.

To be fair, a woman often must struggle
harder than a man simply because more gender
limits are imposed on her than on any man. So?
Just because life may be tough, should a woman
simply accept what comes her way? Most of the
women I know do not, and I bet most of those
you know don't, either.

Nevertheless, our media—our journalism, our
art—abound with wounded women. We seem to
have lost our sturdy immigrant past, forgotten that
we once had strong and gallant women heroes
such as the title character in Willa Cather's *My
Antonia*. We are descendants of brave dames like
these, not a nation of weaklings. Yet eighty-one
years after Antonia, we are offered tales of women
who have been battered. Who have been violated,
molested, or date-raped. Who have been sexually
harassed by swinish co-workers. Whose husbands
have left them (generally for younger, juicier
women) high, dry, and impoverished. Who are
debilitated by obscure ailments. Who are simply
sick to death of life.

Are some of these sad narratives stories of
authentic victims? Of course. Read or watch *The
Color Purple* or *Sophie's Choice*. Read our first literature, the Bible. Dinah, the daughter of Leah and

Jacob, was no wimpette; she was a genuine victim. She was raped. She was powerless. That is, there was nothing she could do to prevent the violence against her. So some victims are genuine victims. The physical pain of domestic violence is real pain. So is the psychic pain of clinical depression.

But are a fair number of these tales actually weepies about women who could have fought for themselves and chose not to? Damn right. A damsel-in-distress, movie-of-the-week mentality has infected our film and fiction. Despite the most recent revolution in women's rights, we are still being portrayed as the gender of the quivering lower lip. Our art, not our lives, too often presents us as the demonstrably weaker sex. Worse, instead of seeing suffering as a condition that morally requires us to respond with pity and aid, too many of us have come to believe that *being* a victim is somehow noble. That kind of thinking leads to a flowering of wimpettes.

Look, who are among this decade's female demigods? Dead Diana. In life, she certainly did speak out for noble causes, but her real vocation was getting friends and journalists to headline her agonies—bulimia, suicide attempts, anguish inflicted by a faithless husband and censorious in-laws—and to report on her attempts at recovery, from standard psychotherapy to all manner of New Age drivel to pumping iron at a gym. Extra! Extra! She got the whole world to read all about it. (That the whole world included her young sons did not slow down the "people's princess" one whit.)

For those cerebral types who found Diana too featherbrained to venerate, there was attorney and Yale Law School alumna Anita Hill to revere. This *über* wimpette testified before Congress how she endured vile sex talk from a superior rather than (1) report him for harassment through established procedures or (2) tell him to shut the hell up.

This canonization of female degradation and malaise is dangerous. It depreciates the suffering of women who truly are victims. It degrades women's views of themselves. Yet the mantle of victimization seems so chic that I expect to see it on the cover of *Vogue*. Everyone wants to try it on. There is an often-cited, unattributed statistic wafting in the media ether and on college campuses these days that a fourth of all American women have been abused or sexually assaulted. Does "abused" mean physically battered? Does it refer to a sex act consummated without a woman's explicit verbal consent but with her implicit agreement? Or is it about something nasty in between? We don't know, yet we renounce skepticism and rush to outrage.

I cannot understand why our art does not

reflect the strong women I meet every day. Now, I'm not saying the dames I know—my friends, my colleagues, my neighbors—are invincible. But pound for pound, they are heartier, more high-spirited, more valorous, and infinitely less frivolous than so many wimpettes we see today in literature, film, and television. Their paradigmatic experience is neither forcible violation nor abuse. Yes, their lives are sometimes tough, but in the worst of times—in the face of illness, death, economic worries, family traumas—they show amazing resilience. I am not talking about Cabinet-level women: I'm talking about nursery school teachers, poets, secretaries, interior decorators, community volunteers. Ordinary citizens. And while we're on the subject, how come when women on-screen or in books *do* manage to act assertively, as in *Thelma and Louise* and *What's Love Got to Do with It,* they are often pitted against one specific evil—bad men? The cosmos gets reduced to gender warfare.

Turn on the TV, read a book, or go to a movie, and you'll find hurt women disturbingly prominent in our art. This worries me. The Big Lie repeated often enough becomes truth. I, for one, don't want to be assumed to be weak or wounded. Further, art not only reflects society, it is society's collective memory: It can become history the way a Supreme Court decision does, by ultimately changing the minds—or at least the behavior—of Americans. Do we want our descendants to look back at the women who bore them as wimpettes? Worse, do we want them to inherit the belief that women are inherently less stalwart than men?

The wimpette's pain may be real, but she does little or nothing to avert it. She *can* act, but chooses not to. Her unspoken credo is this: Women are helpless or close to it. They don't act independently; they react to men and frequently take their identities from the men in their lives. When they do act bravely, it is, even today, often to defend husband, home, hearth, and children, or the community in which said husband, home, and so forth are set. Anne Archer's Beth in *Fatal Attraction* is a prime example. For many wimpettes, the world stops at the white pickets of their fences; they lack the curiosity to look past the spaces between the pickets at the world beyond because they are so self-involved. Larger causes—racial equality, justice—are left to the guys.

Now, while the Bible is still open: The culture that gave rise to the recording of the story of Genesis might have believed as a general proposition that women are weak. But Eve did not have to be. One of the many points of the story of the Temptation is that Eve *could* have said no. Yes, the serpent was persuasive, and the fruit of the Tree of Knowledge must indeed have seemed exceedingly succulent. However, Eve had neither the stature nor the will to even try to fight a cosmic battle. The mother of us all was, sadly, a wimpette.

From Eve on, there have always been women in literature who simply could not cope. Some were real victims, some wimpettes. Of the protagonists who even tried to break the mold, many came to a bad end or died, including Anna Karenina, Tess of the D'Urbervilles, Maggie Tulliver in *The Mill on the Floss*, and Lily Bart in *The House of Mirth*, to name just a few.

Since those times, however, we've had the suffragette movement, the march of women out of the home into the workplace during the wartime forties, and the liberation movement of the sixties and seventies. Yet we still have had a surprising amount of fiction—some of high literary merit, such as Anna Quindlen's *Black and Blue*, Stephen King's *Rose Madder*, and Dorothy Allison's *Bastard Out of Carolina*—that is premised on women suffering under the tyranny of men. (Some is simplistic, cheap victim fiction, third-rate stuff, like the spate of quasiliterate whodunits about serial killers that feature women being tortured, raped, and/or murdered, all attempting—and failing—to emulate *The Silence of the Lambs*. But that novel featured the valiant and virtuous Clarice Starling, as well as author Thomas Harris's brilliant, harrowing insights into the psyche of a maniac. What is literature in *Silence* comes close to misogynistic porn in the descriptions of violence and torment in the work of author James Patterson, to say nothing of the novels of his less able colleagues.)

In film, brave dame Norma Rae has given way to wimpettes Thelma and Louise driving off a cliff. On television, Ally McBeal is a litigator far longer on legs than brains. McBeal proves you can send the girl to college, but not even seven years of higher education can stay her from doing what comes naturally—trying to catch a man. *Juris doctor* or no, the girl can't help it.

At this juncture, it's fair to ask: Why do we need heroic women? Aren't we human? Aren't we flawed? Can't we suffer? Of course we can. Some of the bravest dames are characters who have suffered some wrong and managed to transcend or avenge that injury, like Offred in Margaret Atwood's *A Handmaid's Tale*. Some, like Karen Silkwood, die trying. Heroes can and do get hurt; heroism, after all, is a human quality. Only in the simplistic world of comics is it a superhuman one.

What brave dames have in common is that *they're passionate about something besides passion.* Yes, Jane Eyre loved Edward Rochester, but her life-long quest was not for love but for justice. Brave dames, then, are self-sufficient, active, dynamic, three-dimensional heroes who see past that picket fence. They may love their children, but they also love the work that takes them away from them. They may be interested in men—and often are successful in their relationships with them—but they rarely spend their time mooning over a man. Nor are they full-time victims, either of circumstance or of villains. The message of the movies, books, and television shows they inhabit is that you can care about home and hearth and also the world beyond them. You can do well, do good, or simply do. Brave dames can be strong and active, but they are not only about kicking butt. Like Marge on *The Simpsons*, who is often the lone voice of decency speaking out against her town's and husband's flaming stupidity, they are moral.

So what's the problem? It's not as if we're so recently liberated that we have yet to develop a clear notion of what a female hero should be. The archetype of a strong woman has existed for centuries side by side with wimpettes. Unlike Athena popping out of Zeus's forehead full-grown and armored, strong women did not suddenly emerge from the brow of the estimable Betty Friedan as she sat typing *The Feminine Mystique*.

Brave dames have triumphed over adversity in life and in art since recorded time. Look at the Bible once more: There is the widow Ruth, committed enough to God and her mother-in-law to leave her home and people to embrace a new faith; the beauty queen Esther, risking execution by appearing unbidden before the king to expose the genocidal machinations of Haman; the prophet Deborah, who helped deliver the Israelites from their oppressors, the Canaanites.

Women are as competent and brave as the next guy. Historically, fiction has on occasion provided well-rounded female heroes. I mentioned Jane Eyre before. She is my favorite example of a complex and heroic female character, a brave dame. She had high moral standards, stood up to injustice, and was willing to leave civilization and face the wild, even death, rather than do wrong. Other early brave dames include Jo March in *Little Women*, Elizabeth Bennet in *Pride and Prejudice*, and Eliza in *Uncle Tom's Cabin*. *Gone with the Wind*'s Scarlett O'Hara was not in their league in the ethics department, yet her devotion to the land and her incredible tenacity make her a contender, too.

BRAVE DAME PHILOSOPHY
(actually, the philosophy of any first-rate person, regardless of gender)

Article One: A brave dame is passionate about something besides passion.

Article Two: Even in the worst of times, a brave dame does not give up; she is resilient.

Article Three: A brave dame is competent.

Article Four: A brave dame is willing to face moral and physical challenges.

Article Five: A brave dame has high ethical standards.

Article Six: A brave dame stands up to injustice.

Article Seven: A brave dame is a true friend.

We can find admirable heroes in film and television as well, though we frequently need to look to earlier decades to come up with the best of them. The films of the 1930s and 1940s provide some dandy role models. The year 1939 brought Judy Garland as Dorothy in *The Wizard of Oz* and Vivien Leigh as Scarlett O'Hara in *Gone with the Wind*. The following year gave us Ginger Rogers in *Kitty Foyle*, Jane Darwell in *The Grapes of Wrath*,

Greer Garson in *Pride and Prejudice*, and Katharine Hepburn in *The Philadelphia Story*. My personal top two brave movie dames are Katharine Hepburn in *Adam's Rib* (1949) and Rosalind Russell as intrepid reporter Hildy Johnson (originally written as a male part) in *His Girl Friday* (1940).

Katharine Hepburn's Amanda Bonner is smart, funny, and direct, a Yale Law School graduate and accomplished litigator who is married to Adam Bonner, played by Spencer Tracy. She's passionate in her defense of the astoundingly dumb blonde Doris Attinger (Judy Holliday). In facing off against her husband—who happens to be the assistant district attorney prosecuting the matter—Amanda sets out to prove that his case is a reflection of sexist double standards. Her character pleases on two levels. First, she's a career woman who is also beautiful and appealing—and who isn't neurotic. Second, she's passionate not only about her man, but also about her work and equal rights for women.

Rosalind Russell's character in the romantic comedy *His Girl Friday* is an intrepid crime reporter. She lets the audience know where she stands right at the start of the movie, when a man offers to help her with a meeting. "I can handle it," she quips. She is the one who divorced her boss, not the other way around. And he wants her

SUSAN ISAACS

back, whereas her biggest priority is getting the story. When Hildy's new fiancé protests her involvement in a manhunt, she fires back at him, "Can't you see this is the biggest thing in my life?"

Even the 1950s—a decade marked by movies-to-cringe-by about women mortifying themselves in their pursuit of husbands—produced a few exceptional female characters. *Pat and Mike* (1952) is another Katharine Hepburn vehicle in which she stars as a crack athlete. Dorothy McGuire is a Quaker preacher and pacifist in *Friendly Persuasion* (1956). And two more of my favorites are *All About Eve* (1950), with Bette Davis, and the comedy-satire *Auntie Mame* (1958), starring the ebullient Rosalind Russell.

Film critic Molly Haskell has even argued convincingly that Doris Day, whom many consider a "hundred-watt reminder of the excessively bright and eager-to-please feminine masquerade of the fifties,"[1] was actually "challenging, in her working woman roles [as in *Pillow Talk* (1959) or *Lover Come Back* (1962)], the limited destiny of women to marry, live happily ever after, and never be heard from again."[2]

1. Molly Haskell, *Holding My Own in No Man's Land: Women and Men and Film and Feminists* (New York: Oxford University Press, 1997), p. 22.
2. Ibid., p. 27.

My favorite brave dame from television is Mary Tyler Moore's Mary Richards. There are many courageous women in TV series, such as the protagonists of *Roseanne* and *Ellen*, but their valor, for the most part, is of the everyday sort, meeting challenges with dignity and assertiveness. Genuinely brave dames, women who face moral or physical challenges, such as Pocahontas or private eye Kinsey Milhone, are to be discovered in films and fiction and the occasional TV show like *Dr. Quinn, Medicine Woman* and *Buffy the Vampire Slayer*. However, Mary is the best of the everyday women, so decent and upstanding, such a trailblazer on television, that for me she rates brave dame status even though she does not have to face rattlesnakes or vampires.

Ironically, the brave dames of the past—from nineteenth-century fiction, from films of the 1930s through the 1950s, from 1970s TV—developed in times when women were subjugated, or at least still constrained. Now, however, women have far more social and political muscle. They are free (or at least freer) to be full members of society. So how come the proliferation of wimpettes in our arts? First, the freedom that is exhilarating to some is terrifying to others, who run back to the house and start stitching Home Sweet Home samplers like mad. Second, some artists—male and female—

simply hate women. They will not accord us full humanity. And finally, there are plenty of writers, directors, and actors who lack the imagination or the character to see beyond stereotypes. For all of these, what is a politically acceptable way of keeping women down on the farm, in the house, out of power? Portray them as put-upon, as helpless, as hurt. Turn them into victims.

Today the archetypal modern heroine is a weakened heroine. Sometimes all she does is provide set decoration; moviemakers toss a bone to feminists by giving women bit parts, showing women in judges' robes or surgical scrub suits. More important female characters with perpetually erect nipples now do hold traditionally male jobs, but they don't act like professionals. They're still old-fashioned girls. How many films feature powerful women in starring roles, such as Susan Sarandon as a lawyer in *The Client*? What we get instead is a skimpily clad Nicole Kidman in *Days of Thunder* as a neurosurgeon cheering on her race car driver boyfriend. Or a Cameron Diaz in *There's Something About Mary* as an orthopedic surgeon who is never actually seen in surgery—but who is seen undressing before an open window as if she were either utterly guileless or, despite the buoyant innocence of her character, an exhibitionist. Here, finally, are women who are driving the story, or at least in the front passenger seat. We like them; Kidman and Diaz are as engaging as hell. And they look as if they're going to be brave dames. But they are not Sarandon.

What all of these wimpettes and near-wimpette characters have in common is that they are barely able to transcend their own genitalia. Everything they do proceeds from a single premise: They are women. As a result, they are one-dimensional characters. (Men, on the other hand, are allowed to be interesting and interested. Any of their traits that are not inherently male are still intrinsic to their character. They may be husbands and fathers, for instance, but they're rarely defined by those roles, as with Gregory Peck as Atticus Finch in *To Kill a Mockingbird*. And when they are—as in a perfect-dad movie such as *Kramer vs. Kramer* or *Mrs. Doubtfire*—they're loving, competent, and noble, often in contrast to an unstable or absent woman.)

I DON'T MEAN THAT YOU have to analyze everything you read or see in terms of brave dames and wimpettes. First, all good art, from a Shakespearean tragedy to a Coward comedy, works on many levels. Good art cannot be devalued into being about one particular subject. Besides, a work can be politically incorrect and still have enormous emotional appeal or aesthetic value. Look at the wimpette fairy tale "Cinderella" and its adaptations: Rossini's comic opera *Cenerentola*, Prokofiev's ballet, Disney's animated feature, *Pretty Woman*, and *Ever After: A Cinderella Story*.

And I am definitely *not* suggesting banning or in any way attempting to inhibit the distribution and consumption of certain works of art based on a political litmus test. I treasure the freedoms granted by the First Amendment, including the right of the artist to create whatever art he or she pleases and the right of the reader or viewer to applaud or to yell, "Hey, this stinks in spades!"

What I do believe is that wimpettes are so much with us that we often don't see them for what they are: weak sisters, personifications of antifeminist propaganda, reflections of our lesser selves, refutations of our better selves. I would like us all, myself included, to become more thoughtful critics, smarter consumers of art. Further, in an artistic variant of Gresham's law, the presence of so many wimpette protagonists—faux victims and ersatz madonnas and dumb blondes—drives out brave dames.

S O WHERE ARE JANE EYRE, Amanda Bonner, Hildy Johnson, and Mary Richards at the end of the twentieth century? We have indeed come a long way since the fiction of the nineteenth century, the films of the thirties and forties, and the television of the seventies. Or have we?

In this book, I am watching out for the wimpettes, even those who hide their lights under Sisterhood Is Powerful T-shirts. Specifically, I am focused on what I call the articles of wimpette philosophy.

WIMPETTE PHILOSOPHY

Article One: All men are really little boys at heart.

Article Two: Your worth rises in direct proportion to your masochism.

Article Three: A wimpette always opts for indirection and subterfuge.

Article Four: Men are strong and women are weak.

Article Five: A wimpette has low ethical standards. She is a moral lightweight

except, occasionally, in sexual matters
(and even there her abstinence has to
do with her perceived value to a man
rather than any deeply held belief).
Article Six: A wimpette betrays other
women, including her friends.
Article Seven: A wimpette does not take
responsibility for her own actions and
blames her lack of action on others.
Article Eight: A wimpette looks to a man
to give her an identity.

What I want to find, for me and you, are characters with the spirit of Jane, Amanda, Hildy, and
Mary who are with us today.

2

Women as Wives

*The Little Woman, the Lover,
the Soul Mate, and, of Course,
the Brave Dame and Wimpette*

WHEN WAS THE LAST TIME you saw a
movie in which a husband spent all his
time hanging around the house waiting for his
wife to get home? When an actor plays a husband,
he gets to go outside to strut his stuff. But, though
this is the nineties, the alleged stuff of too many of
the wives in film and on TV is the same old sugar
and spice and everything nice.

There seem to be more single and divorced
women in current fiction and fewer married ones,
but at least these wives are doing better than the
ones on-screen—at least in terms of the complexity and depth of their portrayals. The most memorable have been the strong wives with sad stories:
Beth, the mother of a missing boy in Jacquelyn

Mitchard's *The Deep End of the Ocean*, and Carolyn in Rosellen Brown's elegant, exquisitely painful *Before and After*. In the novel, Carolyn's teenage son is accused of murdering his girlfriend. As the family's lovely life unravels, as Carolyn's husband tries to hide evidence of the boy's guilt, it is she who, despite her anguish, is a seeker after true justice. (The 1996 film version with Meryl Streep, although long-winded, said less.)

Movie and TV wives have not been such finely wrought characters, although some certainly qualify as semibrave dames, not flinching from moral challenges and physical danger. However, their concerns have far less to do with the outside world than with the care of their husbands and families. Far too many are wimpettes, performing modern variations on eyelash fluttering and biceps squeezing: talking cute, talking smart, talking dirty, but ultimately expending their energy being the girls men want them to be.

A corollary is the large number of films—and some television series—in which women, mostly wimpettes, ache to get married. They are exemplars of Article Eight of the Wimpette Philosophy, that a wimpette is a woman who looks to a man to give her an identity. Remember *My Best Friend's Wedding*? *In and Out*? *Wedding Bell Blues*? *Only You*? *Muriel's Wedding*? *Jerry Maguire*? *Once Around*?

We've also had a spate of period films recently in which nice girls are looking for husbands. The best of these husband hunters are in adaptations of Jane Austen's novels. Emma Thompson, intelligent as always, shines as Elinor Dashwood in director Ang Lee's lovely 1995 film *Sense and Sensibility*. (Thompson also wrote the screenplay.) True, there is no doubt Elinor is a creature of her time, an impoverished gentlewoman who knows women have but one hope: marriage. Yet she has strength and spirit and wit, and unlike her modern miniskirted sisters, she would never abase herself to snare a man. Ditto for Gwyneth Paltrow as Miss Woodhouse in writer/director Douglas McGrath's winning *Emma* (1996). (Writer/director Amy Heckerling's delicious 1995 Beverly Hills comedy *Clueless*, with Alicia Silverstone, is based on Austen's *Emma*. *Clueless* is truly contemporary, however, in that its brave dame protagonist is not looking for a husband—although she does find a bright, moral beau who is as worthy of her as she is of him.)

WIMPETTES

But back to wimpettes. Anne Archer and Annabella Sciorra have grabbed the saintly-spouse crown previously held by Myrna Loy in *The Best Years of Our Lives*. In *Fatal Attraction* and *The Hand That Rocks the Cradle*, these two actresses defined for this generation the quintessential good wife and mother. But Loy's battle can at least be construed as a patriotic one—easing the emotional wreck of a warrior back into a life of peace. Granted, that is a woman's role as ancient as Penelope's in *The Odyssey*, but at least it has important social consequences. Archer and Sciorra, on the other hand, are merely defending what is theirs from a female predator.[3] They are modern only in that they reverse the virginal blonde–bad brunette cliché.

Starting with Beth in *Fatal Attraction* (1987), Anne Archer has played a number of wives: Dr. Cathy Ryan in the films of the Clancy books *Patriot Games* (1992) and *Clear and Present Danger* (1994) and, most recently, in the Lifetime movie *Indiscretion of an American Wife* (1998).

In the first three, she was the perfect wife. Beth in *Fatal Attraction*, as Susan Faludi has so perceptively written, has no career and is "the complete Victorian hearth angel (à la the prototypical "Beth" of *Little Women*), sipping tea, caressing

---

3. For more on these films, see chapter 3. For an in-depth discussion of *Fatal Attraction*, see Susan Faludi's book *Backlash* (New York: Doubleday, 1991), pp. 117–23.

piano keys, and applying cosmetics with an almost spiritual ardor."[4] Her only role apart from wife and mother appears to be finding and decorating a house. When she addresses her husband, it's to ask him if her hair looks okay or to drag him away from his flirtation at the bar with femme fatale Alex—or to tell him he's been replaced in their bed for the night by their daughter. For a wimpette such as Beth, this is supposed to pass for assertiveness. Naturally, she takes her husband back despite his infidelity and, ultimately, slays the bunny-boiling Glenn Close.

Do not mistake this last act for one of valor. Beth is no brave dame. Indeed, she is the personification of Article One of the wimpette philosophy, that men are really little boys. This notion allows these women to stay out of the fight for the boys' toys—all that silly old power and autonomy. Instead they stay at home, young, desexualized mommies, and step in only to clean up the boys' messes, be it socks on the floor or the ravages of a malevolent mistress.

Archer continued her career as helpmate to the stars in the Clancy films, though in these she is promoted to surgeon. But her work is perfunctory; she's still really about home and hearth and

4. Ibid., p. 120.

wimpettedom. In the made-for-cable movie *Indiscretion of an American Wife*, however, she is no longer the perfect hausfrau. She has an affair with a vintner, an illustration of the first section of Article Five, which states that a wimpette has low ethical standards. But what all of these roles have in common is that Archer's character is largely defined by being married to a successful man—a lawyer, a CIA agent, and a diplomat. (Both her characters and Annabella Sciorra's also illustrate Article Eight, that a wimpette looks to a man for identity.)

Sciorra as Claire in *The Hand That Rocks the Cradle* is another housebound wife—though she dabbles in botany—who must slay an evil single woman, nanny Peyton (Rebecca De Mornay), who is out to destroy the family. We know Claire is a good spouse because she gets up at four-thirty in the morning to type a proposal for her husband, Michael (Matt McCoy). Frightened and jealous of her husband—who is portrayed as a sensitive and reasonable guy—Claire is forever apologizing to him. Like Beth in *Fatal Attraction*, the only act of bravery for this wimpette comes when she has to kill off the wacko Peyton.

Even before she played Claire, Sciorra was playing wives (Alan Dershowitz's in *Reversal of Fortune* [1990]), girlfriends (of James Woods, in

The Hard Way [1991]), and brides (in *True Love* [1989]). The most interesting role she's had a chance to play is Angie in *Jungle Fever* (1991). There she was also a girlfriend, but at least she had equal billing with her lover, played by Wesley Snipes. Since *The Hand That Rocks the Cradle*, Sciorra has played a cheated-on wife in *Romeo Is Bleeding* (1994) and in *Cop Land* (1997), and a girl-friend in *Mr. Jealousy* (1998). She also plays Robin Williams's wife in *What Dreams May Come* (1998), where she is a woman who commits suicide after her husband's death and must be saved from eternal damnation by her heavenly spouse.

Another wife who must fight and kill the other woman come to wreck her home—like Beth with Alex in *Fatal Attraction* and Claire with Peyton in *The Hand That Rocks the Cradle*—is Barbara Sabich (Bonnie Bedelia), who kills off Carolyn Polhemus (Greta Scacchi) in *Presumed Innocent* (1990). In Scott Turow's splendid first novel, on which the film is based, Barbara is subtly rendered as a woman of strong interests, an in-triguing, twisted character. In the movie, Bedelia does give a good performance, and at least her character is less sympathetic and attractive than the sweetie pies Beth and Claire. Like them, however, she is battling a threatening single woman. While the wives in the films *Fatal Attraction* and *Presumed*

Innocent are bright enough, the evil female rival is not only sexier but, perhaps more cruelly, more successful.

What is all this lady-killing about, anyway? We do love a happy ending, good triumphing over evil, so what could be happier and more American than a villainess getting hers? But these murders also underscore the wimpettes' secret desire to annihilate the brave dames they can't be. Brilliant women, erotic women, scheming women, and powerful women are so threatening by virtue of the simple fact that they exist that they cannot be allowed to live. In specific movies they do indeed menace the marriage or the family. But what they are truly threatening is our entire culture, in which men are men and women are still girls. The wimpettes kill off these defiant women on behalf of themselves and the audience.

Sometimes the conflict is less confrontational, as with Mary Ann (Charlize Theron) against the hellhound Christabella (Connie Nielsen) in *The Devil's Advocate*; Susan Hendler (Caroline Goodall) against Meredith Johnson (Demi Moore) in *Disclosure*; Carla Brigance (Ashley Judd) against Ellen Roark (Sandra Bullock) in *A Time to Kill*; and Abby McDeere (Jeanne Tripplehorn) against a beach temptress in *The Firm*. With the exception of *The Firm*, the enemy in these films is also a single, ball-busting career woman, so unlike the poor, innocent wives with whom we are supposed to sympathize. (And often we do. We've all been brought up on books and movies and TV shows in which simple is better than complex, klutzy is more appealing than skillful, and wide, trusting eyes are far more inviting than a skeptical raised eyebrow—at least where women are concerned.)

In *Devil's Advocate* (1997), Charlize Theron plays Mary Ann, the fragile-flower wife of Kevin Lomax (Keanu Reeves), a hotshot young defense lawyer. Though at one point she says this is the first time she hasn't worked since she was thirteen, all Mary Ann is seen doing—before she has a breakdown—is sitting around at home, decorating their stunning co-op and congratulating Kevin for his great work and for making so much money. Mary Ann is the stereotypical wimpette: She is aggressively unworldly, which in Hollywood's view is somehow always endearing, never tedious. When the couple attends a Manhattan party so icily sophisticated it would scare the hell out of most Manhattanites, she is desperate for Kevin not to leave her side. She then confides her miseries in Kevin's boss John Milton (Al Pacino as the Devil), whom she has only just met; all dewy with gulli-bility, she takes his advice about how to wear her hair. Her childishness is presented as an asset. She's the lamb, the guileless rube, i.e., in the film's terms, the ideal woman.

In *Disclosure* (1994), based on Michael Crichton's novel, Tom Sandler (Michael Douglas reprising his husband-as-sexual-dweeb role from *Fatal Attraction*) is married to wimpette Susan (Caroline Goodall), a lawyer now home with the kids. (In the book, she's working four days a week.)

We see Susan driving Tom to get his ferry, discussing what kind of Barbie to get her daughter, as if with each birth she dropped twenty points of IQ. Later, after Tom sues his superior, Meredith Johnson (Demi Moore), for sexual harassment, Susan spends several humiliating scenes sitting through a mediation during which her husband's sexual encounter with his boss is described in graphic detail.

When things start to get hairy for Tom, plucky Susan offers to go back to work full time. His response: "I'm perfectly capable of supporting our family." The implication—vintage Eisenhower era—is that he's not a man if his wife is working. Naturally, she drops the idea immediately. Later, when Susan is worried that Tom's shouting will wake up the children, he says, "Yeah, my children that I provide for and protect," as though she has no role in it.

Further, when successful (read evil) Meredith

sees a photo of Susan and quips that "she looks like she always has food in the refrigerator," Tom, looking embarrassed, mutters something about Susan gaining a few pounds during her pregnancy. This illustrates Article Two of the wimpette philosophy (your worth rises in direct proportion to your masochism); the subservient, the compliant, and the mocked are morally superior to those men and women who don't appreciate them, who are out there in the world having fun.

In *A Time to Kill* (1996), a film based on John Grisham's first novel, Carla Brigance (Ashley Judd), the blond, luscious wife of honey-haired, luscious Jake Brigance (Matthew McConaughey), spends much of the film sitting around their un-air-conditioned Mississippi house barely clad, her skin gleaming with perspiration. She is the perfect sex object, perpetually moist, forever ready, eternally passive. Her adversary, the less sweaty, more energetic, dark-haired Ellen Roark (Sandra Bullock), is from the North. She attends law school at Ole Miss, Carla's alma mater, but she immediately makes it clear to Jake that, unlike his wife, she's no sorority sister. The casting in *A Time to Kill* is so *Archie* comics, so good-Betty and bad-Veronica, that the women might as well be cartoons.

While Roark is bouncing legal theories off

Jake, Carla is at home. The only times she gets out is to go to church and to a barbecue with her family—and to go home to her parents'. And when she says anything, it's usually to complain about Jake's work and how much time it's taking him away from her and their daughter.

Roark, on the other hand, is part of the action. She plans legal strategy with the boys, steals the files of an expert witness, and is abducted by the Klan. She and Jake also spend a good part of the movie flirting wildly and trying womanfully and manfully not to have sex.

Carla never finds out about Jake and Roark. Jake never suffers any consequences for his flirtation. Right on the heels of one of several scenes in which Jake wants to kiss Roark, Carla pops up to tell her husband that she's forgiven him for taking on such a big case, that she understands now why he did it, and that she loves him. Wimpette all the way.

Abby McDeere (Jeanne Tripplehorn) in *The Firm* (1993), another Grisham adaptation, is a wife and schoolteacher who gets to participate in the action—a little. She's smart and, from the start, knows there's something fishy about the law firm her husband, Mitch (Tom Cruise), is dying to join. When her suspicions turn out to be justified, Mitch is the one who takes his fellow partners down. Like Tom Sandler in *Disclosure*, Mitch doesn't let his wife in on his plan initially.

Toward the end of the film, Abby does get to help Mitch out. But while he's jumping from tall buildings, running through traffic, and bringing the mob to its knees, she is using what appears to be her only weapon, her feminine wiles, to ensnare the firm's evil ringleader.

Wimpettes always opt for indirection and subterfuge. (That's Article Three of their philosophy.) Abby chooses to help Mitch without telling him she is doing so, even though she has just found out that he cheated on her on a business trip—a dalliance planned by slimeball Avery and to which Mitch confesses when he realizes Abby will find out about it from the firm. Though Abby's actions can be interpreted as a form of revenge—her secret help gives her power over him—she also can be seen as yet another wimpette wife who stands by her man in the face of his faithlessness.

(Despite Carla Brigance and Abby McDeere, author Grisham has created two marvelous brave dames in other novels. Neither of them is a wife. They are lawyers: Darby Shaw, played by Julia Roberts in the film adaptation of *The Pelican Brief*, and Reggie Love, played by Susan Sarandon in *The Client*, are interesting, appealing characters on page and screen.)

Many feminists were deeply moved by Ada (Holly Hunter) in the Oscar-nominated *The Piano* (1993)—one of my all-time bottom-ten movies. She's cheating on her spouse instead of the other way around. There was great sympathy for this adulteress at the end of the movie, but to my mind she is yet another wimpette.

Ada travels from Scotland to New Zealand with her young daughter to wed Stewart (Sam Neill) in an arranged marriage. The couple never develops any relationship, and before long the mute Ada is having a passionate affair with George (Harvey Keitel). It begins with his extortionate demand, which essentially comes down to "If you let me play with you, I'll let you play that piano you love so much." This is Article Two—your worth rises in direct proportion to your masochism—loud and clear, because it is this act, not of love but of blackmail, that makes her come alive.

What this pseudofeminist film is really saying is that Ada—like Thelma in *Thelma and Louise*—just needs to get laid. And what if Ada doesn't seem to want what's good for her? Force it on her. And sure enough, she does love it. She can't seem to get enough (although not without paying dearly for it with one of her piano-playing fingers— severed with an ax by her vengeful husband).

FIRST LADIES IN FILM TEND to be wimpettes— they play a largely symbolic role, are totally dependent on their husbands for their identities, and bide their time gazing adoringly at the president (or thinking of him from afar, if they happen to be separated). Picture Mary McDonnell in *Independence Day* (1996) and Wendy Crewson in *Air Force One* (1997).

Mary McDonnell's character is so self-effacing that she maintains her First Lady smile through a painful injury, even while she's dying. And the film barely notes her death. The president (Bill Pullman), who is supposedly madly in love with his wife, moves on to fight evil as though nothing much has changed in his life. Sure, it's crunch time on planet Earth, but he can't even make time for a small sob, a slight lump in the throat, a glance heavenward (to the late missus, not to the extra-terrestrials). The very next day he and his daughter are whooping it up after the world is saved, looking as if everything is utterly hunky-dory.

Even when the First Lady is married to a difficult president (and played by a splendid actress, such as Sigourney Weaver in *Dave*, Joan Allen in *Nixon*, and First Lady–to-be Emma Thompson in *Primary Colors*), she still spends a lot of time putting on a good show of it, although perhaps that is the job description.

Primary Colors (1998) is adapted from Joe Klein's thinly veiled, mean-spirited roman à clef about President Clinton's 1992 campaign for the White House. (Neither novel nor movie can be counted as a true work of imagination, as they cannot stand on their own merits. If the Clintons had never been, the book would not have been published and the movie never made. Rather, the works are hybrids of fiction, insider "knowledge," and voyeuristic pandering to a public whose need to know stops at nothing.) In the film the Clinton character, Jack Stanton (John Travolta), has a quickie with a librarian he meets at a campaign stop. Moments later, wife Susan (Emma Thompson) walks into the room full of campaign aides as the disheveled librarian walks out. Clueless Susan is not, but it is nonetheless one of many humiliating scenes she's put through, including the most famous one, a rendition of the *60 Minutes* show during which Hillary Rodham Clinton announced she was not some little Tammy Wynette kind of wife. Admittedly, the movie is more thoughtful than the novel, but both are as painful as the reality—although infinitely less interesting.

Other characters who are devoted wives to rich and/or important men—similar to the First Lady role, only married to, say, a tycoon or a successful lawyer instead of the president—include trophy wife Mickey (Elle Macpherson) in *The Edge* (1997); Kate (Rene Russo) in *Ransom* (1996); and Sarah Turner (Annette Bening) in *Regarding Henry* (1991).

My favorite wimpette in this category is Kathleen Quinlan as Marilyn Lovell in the Oscar-nominated film *Apollo 13* (1995), the astronaut's wife who, in fact, could be confused with a First Lady, so adoring is she. The only difference is that she spends most of the movie in front of a television screen instead of beside her man. And when she's not glued to the tube, she gets the challenging work of telling her husband's mother that there may be a problem on Apollo 13 or announcing that reporters who want to camp out on her lawn can take up their issues with her husband. Yes, this is a true story from the sixties, but I had a personality in the sixties, and if you are old enough to have been alive then, so did you. (And I bet so did Marilyn Lovell.) The filmmakers could at least have given her a little life of her own.

NEAR-WIMPETTES AND
SEMIBRAVE DAMES

Every now and then a film provides a sympathetic portrayal of an adulterous wife, in the mold of *Brief Encounter* (and its 1984 remake, *Falling in Love*, with Meryl Streep). In *Hannah and Her Sisters* (1986), Lee (Barbara Hershey) cheats not on a husband but a boyfriend—with her sister's husband. Even despite this morally iffy behavior, she's a sympathetic character, intelligent and vulnerable.

In the adultery sweepstakes, a few semi-brave dames are sneaking in among the wimpettes. True, they still adhere to Article Eight of the wimpette philosophy and find themselves through men, but at least they reject Article Seven and take responsibility for their behavior. There is Meryl Streep as 1960s housewife Francesca Johnson in *The Bridges of Madison County* (1995), Kristin Scott Thomas as Katharine Clifton in *The English Patient* (1996) and as editor Annie MacLean in *The Horse Whisperer* (1998), and Gwyneth Paltrow in *A Perfect Murder* (1998).

In *The Bridges of Madison County*, based on the Robert Waller best-seller, Francesca is a mother of two and a good but frustrated wife to a passionless husband. She keeps a sparkling clean house on an Iowa farm. She's a little Betty Crocker/passive-aggressive for my taste, but nevertheless a decent human being.

When Francesca's family leaves for four days to attend a state fair, she meets *National Geographic* photographer and master of flowery prose Robert Kincaid (Clint Eastwood). Around him she is by turns womanly and girlish and even a little shy, though not for long. They have a brief but passionate affair. Both realize they have met their soul mate.

Robert is ready to take Francesca away with him, but she ultimately chooses to stay for her family. Also, she realizes their relationship would cease to be special if she were to follow him. Though at times she's a mite servile and overeager for his approval and affection, Francesca is a semi-brave dame and not a wimpette because she usually conducts herself with dignity. She has the audience's sympathy as an Italian-born woman stuck on an Iowa farm for the rest of her life in a dull marriage.

Francesca's affair is not a cheap dalliance. It is with the man she feels she was destined to be with—and one who reciprocates her feelings. Though Robert clearly has been with many women, it is Francesca to whom his attorney sends his personal belongings after his death. They are committing a single immoral act; they are not immoral or self-centered people. Their affair isn't a one-night stand, like Mitch McDeere's in *The Firm* or Dan Gallagher's in *Fatal Attraction*, or an office fling, like Rusty Sabich's in *Presumed Innocent* or Tom Sandler's in *Disclosure*. For all that, I do find it disappointing that Francesca whipped up her courage only to have a brief encounter rather than confront her potato-faced husband.

Annie MacLean (Kristin Scott Thomas) in *The Horse Whisperer* (1998), based on the Nicholas Evans novel, manages to cover three negative stereotypes in a single movie. She's a mean boss, a neglectful mother, and a bad wife. Annie begins as a short-tempered, high-powered career shrew who is working one weekend at the magazine she edits when her daughter has a dreadful riding accident at home. The experience causes Annie to pack up her work and drive her injured daughter and horse across the country to see animal trainer Tom Booker (Robert Redford), a "horse whisperer." She leaves her husband behind in New York.

It takes just a few days at the ranch for Annie to morph miraculously into the opposite extreme of her New York self—a simpering, weepy, besotted wimpette. She's fired from the magazine and falls in love with Tom—so much so that when her husband, Robert (Sam Neill), arrives for a visit, she can hardly keep from making out with Tom in front of her spouse and a roomful of others.

Annie finds herself in the same this-only-happens-once-in-a-lifetime predicament as Francesca. She chooses the harder path of leaving the relationship at a couple of stolen kisses. Like Francesca, she returns to her family. This act of morality and backbone saves her from being a total wimpette.

In the Oscar-winning *The English Patient* (1996), adapted from Michael Ondaatje's novel, Kristin Scott Thomas plays British beauty Katharine Clifton, a married woman in Egypt during World War II who has a passionate affair with Count Laszlo Almasy (Ralph Fiennes). As with the other women discussed here, this is no casual fling, but rather a relationship with the love of her life.

Katharine starts out in brave dame territory, a glamorous and spirited Renaissance woman who flies planes, sings, paints, swims, has a good sense of humor, and is a mesmerizing storyteller. No prima donna, she's often the only woman among men on various expeditions in the desert, and she commands their respect. She's calm under pressure and has no problem camping out with the guys—or when her husband leaves her in the desert with them. Unfortunately, once the affair begins, we rarely see the adventurous side of Katharine. She descends into wimpette territory. She's either performing her social duties or in bed with Almasy. And, despite her physical courage and stamina, her life ultimately comes close to being defined by her relationships with the two men in her life.

The 1998 film *A Perfect Murder* is a remake of Hitchcock's *Dial M for Murder* (1954), which was itself an adaptation of Frederick Knott's spine-tingling play. Like Ada in *The Piano*, Emily Taylor (Gwyneth Paltrow) is somewhat justified in her adultery, being married to a no-good rat, although it seems to me that a truly brave dame would eradicate the pest more honorably through a dissolution of the marriage contract rather than a betrayal of it.

In any case, Emily is the independently wealthy young wife of middle-aged bond trader Steven (Michael Douglas, reprising his oleaginous Gordon Gekko role in *Wall Street*). When Steven finds out about his wife's affair with artist/con artist David, he offers David half a million bucks to kill her.

This premise allows Paltrow to play a victim for most of the film, though she is permitted a healthy amount of leeway in that role. She starts out unknowing (understandably having no idea her lover is a convicted criminal), but she's also well educated and worldly (she works at the UN in a job that requires her to know many languages and to interact with the U.S. ambassador), resourceful (she ultimately figures out her husband is about to lose his shirt and set her up), brave (she tracks down a lead in Washington Heights, though wearing thousands of dollars' worth of jewelry and clothing on the subway may be the act more of a jackass than of a hero), and even deceitful (she lies to Steven, and not only about her affair).

Shirley MacLaine as Tess Carlisle is another semibrave dame, another wife of an important man. She gives a different spin to the First Lady role in *Guarding Tess* (1994). In it, she's a crusty, widowed former First Lady, a difficult old woman, the opposite of the *Independence Day/Air Force One* model. Imperious and short-tempered, she is a public woman who no longer has a public, who has learned how truly expendable a wife can be. Tess's relationship with Secret Service agent Doug Chesnic (Nicolas Cage), while definitely not romantic, is one of intense feeling.

Althea Leasure (Courtney Love) in *The People vs. Larry Flynt* (1996) is also a spouse of a hotshot, but no one would compare her to a First Lady. Uncouth and slovenly, she lacks all decorum. Yes, she's playing a wife, but at least she has a personality—a loud, brash, bisexual, and funny one at that. She's more bravado than bravery, but clearly no wimpette.

Whitney Houston's Julia in *The Preacher's Wife*

(1996) is the energetic, strong-willed wife of Henry (Courtney B. Vance), a beleaguered minister. Though she is a wife and mother, she also sings and directs the church choir and children's pageant. And she—not her husband or the angel who appears to her (Denzel Washington)—drives the story here.

WHEN WOMEN IN FILM, TELEVISION, and fiction aren't defending some threat to home and hearth, they're often standing up to abuse. As I mentioned in chapter 1, stories about victims of battering and abusive husbands and boyfriends are common. They appear in movies such as *Unhook the Stars* (1996), *Boys on the Side* (1995), *This Boy's Life* (1993), *Sleeping with the Enemy* (1991), and *In the Best Interest of the Child* (1990). The topic is popular in TV movies-of-the-week and made-for-cable fare, like the Lifetime movie *The Abduction* and *Lies of the Heart: The Story of Laurie Kellogg* (1994). In other abuse films, a mother must act to protect a child from a father's abuse, as in Lifetime's *Her Desperate Choice* (1998).

Two battered-wife stories stand out because they treat the subject of abuse intelligently and thoughtfully. Their protagonists are brave, although in a domestic setting. In *What's Love Got to Do with It* (1993), Angela Bassett plays rock diva Tina Turner with a focus on her marriage to Ike Turner, who physically and verbally abuses her. Tina Turner shows her courage when she finally leaves Ike, bloodied and with thirty-two cents in her pocket.

Another fine work about an abused woman is Anna Quindlen's recent novel *Black and Blue* (1998). Its heroine, Fran Benedetto, is extraordinarily brave. After years of beatings from her husband, Bobby, Fran flees her house without knowing where she's going, taking her ten-year-old son with her. Her only contact is a woman from a domestic abuse group who helps start new lives for victims of violence. Fran can have no interaction with anyone from her old life, and she and her son must take on completely new identities. Despite the great risk that something will go wrong—and even after her husband manages to track them down—Fran and her son are able to survive and have a normal life again.

TELEVISION SITCOMS CONTINUE TO FEATURE wives in traditional domestic roles such as

Ruth Lucas (Phylicia Rashad) in *Cosby*—though nowadays these women are more likely to have concerns beyond home and hearth. Ruth and her partner (Madeline Kahn) run a neighborhood coffee bar. Jill Taylor (Patricia Richardson) on *Home Improvement* works part time, as does Debra (Patricia Heaton) on *Everybody Loves Raymond*.

Recent sitcoms have also produced wife characters who have equal billing—if not equal status—with their husbands, women such as kooky, quirky, happy-go-lucky flower child Dharma Finkelstein (Jenna Elfman) on *Dharma and Greg* and smart, warm, and grounded Jamie Buchman (Helen Hunt) on *Mad About You*.

On the generally wonderful *Mad About You*, Jamie's husband, Paul (Paul Reiser), has a relatively steady career as a filmmaker. However, Jamie is less certain about what she wants to do. Over the course of six seasons, she works at a corporate job she hates, goes back to school, opens her own PR firm with her best friend, works at the mayor's tourism office, is a campaign manager on a mayoral campaign, and finally goes to work for James Carville and Mary Matalin. It's hard to determine if this is supposed to be some character quirk or is a result of some feud among the show's writers. She may not qualify as a brave dame, but

Jamie is no wimpette: She cares about the world beyond her home and hearth.

Dharma, unfortunately, appears to have hardly any life outside her marriage. Though she's intelligent and energetic, she has no real career (she does teach yoga) and devotes herself to making her husband (Thomas Gibson) happy. She gets him the perfect shower so that he'll feel comfortable in their new home, introduces him to yoga so that he won't be so stressed (he, of course, does substantive work—as an assistant U.S. attorney), and even spends a lot of time placating his difficult mother, to whom she reveals, "It's my job to keep my husband happy."

Dharma also devotes ample time to appreciating Greg's efforts in the sack. She slips into cutesy-poo wimpettespeak in one episode to announce, "I would like to propose a toast to my husband, Greg Montgomery, who works his butt off to put away a bunch of really bad guys—and still has the energy to come home and make hot jungle love to his wife."[5]

5. For an excellent discussion of *Dharma and Greg* (and *Veronica's Closet* and *Ally McBeal*), see Ruth Shalit, "Canny and Lacy," *The New Republic,* Apr. 6, 1998.

BRAVE DAMES

SHE'S NOT EXACTLY A WIFE. In fact, she *has* a wife. Nevertheless, Barbra Streisand as the title character in *Yentl* (1983), based on the Isaac Bashevis Singer story, is a brave dame. In an Orthodox community in Poland where women simply are not permitted to study the Torah—the five books of Moses—and its commentaries, Yentl disguises herself as a man. She burns to learn. This musical about a woman's intellectual and sexual heat and how she channels that heat deserves a mention in this chapter, even if that woman is a husband.

The only actual wife who even comes close to being a truly brave dame is Jamie Lee Curtis as Helen, a twice-duped wife and legal secretary, in James Cameron's *True Lies* (1994). She believes that Harry (Arnold Schwarzenegger), her husband of fifteen years and a spy, is a computer salesman and that Simon (Bill Paxton), a car salesman she meets, is a spy. Once she learns the truth about both, though, she too becomes part of the action.

Helen is so appealing because although she starts out ignorant of skulduggery, she wants to be in on the excitement from the instant she catches on. The reason she falls for Simon's act is that she is aching for adventure. And by the end of the film, she has become an agent teamed with Harry.

Alas, director Cameron trumps up a reason to have Helen dance half naked: She poses as a prostitute who dances for a man she doesn't realize is her husband, Harry. As nearly every critic rightly pointed out, this is not only gratuitous sex, it also slows down the movie.

In addition, when Helen does get to join the guys, she doesn't get to be as brave as they are. Harry blows away one bad guy after another, but the only time her gun goes off is when it falls down some stairs. When Helen finally gets to fight, it's a catfight (snore city) with another woman. And her husband has to rescue her twice, once from Simon and later when she's trapped in a moving car.[6]

A T THE BEGINNING OF THE seventeenth century, in an essay entitled "Of Marriage and Single Life," Francis Bacon wrote: "Wives are young men's mistresses, companions for middle age, and old men's nurses." At the end of the twentieth century, too many writers and directors still find this a dandy definition.

6. For more on *True Lies*, see Caryn James, "The Woman in 'True Lies,' a Mouse That Roared," *The New York Times,* July 17, 1994.

3

Women as Mothers

I'M CRAZY ABOUT MOTHERHOOD. My children, now adults, are as precious to me today as the moment I first held them, seconds after their birth. So if it's such a swell institution, you might ask, how come not one of the brave dames I revere is a mother? Mary Tyler Moore in *The Mary Tyler Moore Show*, Katharine Hepburn in *Adam's Rib*, and Rosalind Russell in *His Girl Friday* are childless. Jane Eyre—to my mind the best of them—has children only in the denouement of the novel, after she's proven how valiant she is. It's not as if I am unacquainted with mother characters; I am. I just never could find any as admirable as my icons.

Why should that be? Well, part of the reason is that throughout literature and film, *mother* has so often been equated with *madonna*. Mary, immaculately conceived, untainted by original sin, beyond sexuality, became the standard for the good mother. But in art, there's a problem with mother characters being ever-loving, unceasingly good. They aren't real women. Virtuous? Indeed. Interesting? No.

Nevertheless, we read and saw too many mothers as self-abnegating saints, like Barbara Stanwyck in *Stella Dallas*. A woman was either a perfect mother or a monster. She could be an ice woman, as Beth Jarrett was in Judith Guest's novel *Ordinary People*. She could also be an out-and-out devil-woman, like Jessica Lange's Martha in the film *Hush* (1998), who tampers with her son's girlfriend's diaphragm and arranges to have the girl subjected to an attempted rape. Sometimes the monster mom's destructiveness was softened by satire and comedy, as in Philip Roth's novel *Portnoy's Complaint* or in films such as *Flirting with Disaster* and *My Favorite Year*. (Part of the power of works such as Frank McCourt's memoir *Angela's Ashes* and William Styron's *Sophie's Choice* was, beyond their brilliance, their novelty. They portrayed mothers neither as perfect nor as fatally flawed, but as troubled human beings.)

But when it comes to creating brave dames, here is the problem with the madonna/monster dichotomy: If a mother on page or screen is a saint, she is always good. There is no need for her to transcend her own limitations or to dare step over the line from safety into danger because, by definition, she is *always* devoted to her family. Her only goal is to do for them—or die for them. The good mother can never be a truly brave dame because there are no challenges for her. She is already perfect.

In life, we mothers are allowed, on occasion, to lapse into flakiness or even indifference and still be thought of as good parents. In art? Forget it. If a mother is less than utterly devoted, she is depicted as putting her children's minds, souls, and very lives at risk. Who but a monster would do such a thing to young innocents?

Make-believe mothers ought to be reflecting what we now acknowledge real mothers—real women—to be: complex beings with rich inner lives, people capable of a range of behavior from egotism to selflessness, from cowardice to valor. Certainly they should be more than either a June Cleaver or a Mrs. Bates.

Well, some are. Some single mothers, particularly on the small screen, are not doing badly these days. But are these good mothers, married and single, brave dames? To the extent many of the good mothers are committed to anything, it is to their children. That is their life's work. They are both defined and limited by their motherhood. When they do act courageously, they often seem less than brave because their acts of valor are portrayed as "natural." They just can't stop themselves from doing good. It is pure instinct, or estrogen, like a lioness protecting her cub. They cannot grow, become better people, or increase in moral stature. Thus, while it may be reassuring to read about or see a mother who can't refrain from being a mini-Mary, it doesn't make for a rich character or convincing art.

WIMPETTES

We love to believe in mother love, that women cannot help but dote on their children. So when women fail to nurture, their behavior shocks because it shakes the foundation not just of our culture, but of our own sense of security. Some of the mothers here are downright bad, and some are simply wimpettes of the first water.

Caroline Wolff (Ellen Barkin), Tobias Wolff's (Leonardo DiCaprio) fifties mother in the film adaptation of the latter's memoir *This Boy's Life* (1993), is a classic wimpette, maternal division. Caroline tries to be a good mother—she plays I Spy with her son and marries a lying, sadistic sicko thinking it will bring her and Toby a more stable life. (Caroline would not get an A-plus in logic.)

Caroline's husband, Dwight (Robert De Niro), abuses both Toby and Caroline verbally and, eventually, physically. Caroline can't and won't stand up to him or anyone else until the very end of the film, when she finally musters the courage to leave. For the better part of two hours, she sits—usually sewing—while Dwight tortures her son. She is a clear illustration of Article Two of the wimpette philosophy, that your worth rises in direct proportion to your masochism, and also of Article Seven, that a wimpette does not take responsibility for her own actions.

Mainstream mothers-to-be often are defined almost entirely by their impending motherhood, as if the growing fetus is taking up the energy previously used for thought. They seem to be abandoning all concern for the world outside home and hearth; occasionally their world does not extend at all beyond their uteruses. It's a reversion to the cliché about women being meant to make babies— and not much more. In *Nine Months* (1995), though Rebecca (Julianne Moore) is also a schoolteacher, the focus is on her pregnancy, as suggested by the movie's title. And *Nine Months* ends with the obligatory labor scene, with not just one but two women giving birth (Joan Cusack, as the sister-in-law who already has children, is the other).

In *Father of the Bride Part II* (1995), again, there's not one but two pregnant mothers (Diane Keaton and Kimberly Warner), one of whom is mother to the other. The message is: Young or old, this is what women do. Mary Steenburgen's character in *Parenthood* (1989) is a mother of three with another on the way. Her character, like Diane Keaton's in *Father of the Bride Part II*, is defined by her relationships with her husband and her kids and by her pregnancy.

Marisa Tomei, who was so zesty as Mona Lisa Vito in *My Cousin Vinny*, waddles through *The Paper* (1994) as Martha Hackett, who is eight and a half months pregnant while her husband, Henry, a newspaper editor (Michael Keaton), pursues a hot story. A reporter on maternity leave, Marty is miserable not working—and terrified of what her future holds—and helps her husband get the story. She rails against women whose professional lives end once they bear children, yet she spends much of the movie as a nagging pregnant wife. A wimpette.

W IMPETTES WHO ARE ALSO MONSTER moms, women who personify Article

Seven—a wimpette does not take responsibility for her actions—regularly appear on made-for-TV movies and miniseries, often "based on actual events," like *Willing to Kill: The Texas Cheerleader Story* (1992); *High Stakes* (1997; mother with a gambling addiction); and *Chasing the Dragon* (1996; mother with a drug addiction). They appear in series dramas such as *Beverly Hills 90210* (Kelly's mom, Jackie Taylor Silver, is an alcoholic), *Sisters* (the sisters' mother, Beatrice, also drinks to excess), and *ER* (Susan Lewis's sister, Chloe, is a drug addict).

Sometimes abusing mothers are not substance abusers; their badness is more insidious. In *Mother* (1996), Debbie Reynolds plays Beatrice, beneath whose cheery mien lurks a harpy to whom all of her writer son John's (Albert Brooks) problems are attributable. (In 1996's *The Mirror Has Two Faces*, Lauren Bacall as Hannah is the Jewish mother who is to blame for her daughter's problems.) It's a rare moment when Beatrice isn't embarrassing John or nagging him about something—his weight, his hair, his shoes, his clothes, his eating habits. She's embarrassed about him, too, as when she lies to her friends about his writing. And she makes clear that she prefers John's younger brother to him. It turns out that Beatrice wanted to be a writer herself but sacrificed that goal to take care of her boys. This character is a mistress of masochism and thus a walking embodiment of Article Two—and an anti-Semitic caricature to boot. Feh.

Mrs. Costanza (Estelle Harris), George's mother on *Seinfeld*, is one bad mother who is wildly funny. She is married to the equally irascible, hilarious Frank, and George's many problems can be assumed to be traceable to both. Mrs. Costanza, in her own berserk way, comes closer to being a brave dame than a wimpette. She never insinuates; she confronts. She doesn't speak in honeyed tones; she screeches what she wants.

MALEVOLENT MOMS ARE USUALLY PRESENTED as either sick, defective, or plain old evil, since a "normal" mother would be a madonna. Yet, rotten as they are, these characters are often far more memorable than all those saintly mothers, and not just because we're gripped by their pathology. They seem so much more alive because we can glimpse real feelings. Ugly feelings, definitely, but at least those are more credible than the eternal furrowed brow of maternal concern, the egregious, tedious benevolence of so many of the maternal wimpettes we meet in our art.

But some of these bad mothers disturb us not only because they're rotten to the core. We sense they're more than mere villains. Iago in *Othello* and Darth Vader in *Star Wars* are evil *individuals*. They never stand for the iniquity of any group, diabolical Venetians or Jedi knights. Yet while destructive mother characters do shine from within with their own vileness, they also make us uncomfortable because they are illuminated from without—by our culture's misogyny. I don't think it is a coincidence that J. R. R. Tolkien's giant spider in *The Two Towers* who devours her offspring is named *She*lob (emphasis mine).

This is not to say that good art can't feature bad mothers. But when a character is well drawn, we sense she does not stand for all womankind, or all working-class women, or all Jewish women. She is neither a brave dame nor a wimpette. She is simply bad to the bone. In *The Grifters* (1990), for example, Anjelica Huston plays Lilly, a con artist. After killing her son's girlfriend, she tries to steal her son's cash. When he catches her, she tries every trick in her book to get the money—including suggesting she's not his mother and coming on to him. Finally, she kills him. Lilly is truly no good, but she's a swell character.

A brief digression: The true monster is in a

small but memorable class of her own. The wicked queen from "Snow White" and the heartless step-mother from "Cinderella" stay with us. The evil Kate in the John Steinbeck novel *East of Eden*, Raymond's mother in Richard Condon's *The Manchurian Candidate* (played by Jo Van Fleet and Angela Lansbury, respectively, in the screen versions), Joan Crawford (Faye Dunaway) in *Mommie Dearest*, and Mary Tyler Moore in *Ordinary People* will remain in our memories into the next century.

NEAR-WIMPETTES AND SEMIBRAVE DAMES

Ever since the seventies, as more women began to leave their children for the day and go to work, to view themselves as part of a world beyond home and hearth, America's passion to see mothers being good has grown. Therefore, when a mother gives less than 100 percent in a book or film or on TV, terrible things happen to her family, as if this is the penalty she pays for allowing herself to take pleasure in life away from her family.

Despite its title, the movie *The Good Mother* (1988), based on Sue Miller's novel, is in fact about a "bad" mother who gets punished. Diane Keaton as Anna gives a solid performance as the single working mother of Molly. She works to support her daughter, though, not for herself. When she's accused of not being passionate about her job at a lab, she responds that she's passionate about Molly, committed to putting food on the table, and not good at anything.

When Anna meets Leo, played by Liam Neeson, she has a sexual awakening. (Who wouldn't?) The two of them take Molly into their bed with them one night and, thinking she's asleep, make love. Molly tells her father, and Anna winds up in a bitter court battle that ends with her losing Leo and custody of her daughter.

Though Anna talks about her independence and being her own person, she's also a victim—of the wrong lawyer, the wrong judge, and a court system ill-suited to handle this kind of case. In wimpette fashion, she meekly accepts her miserable plight, selling out Leo in the process, although she is not a total wimpette, like Caroline in *This Boy's Life*, because she is genuinely devoted to her child, not paralyzed by her own masochism.

The Anna of Sue Miller's novel is a far richer creation, both as a mother and a sexual being. Here too there are no easy answers, but because in the book it is easier to understand Anna's compromises, the reader feels more compassion and less frustration than the viewer.

B RAVE DAMES HAVE TO RISE to meet extraordinary challenges. Going to work is not
sufficient to qualify; it is now a commonplace in
American life and television. So while some of the
mothers on TV are exemplary citizens, they are
merely strong women, not brave dames.

Though stay-at-home mothers such as Cindy
Walsh (Carol Potter) on *Beverly Hills 90210* and the
two mothers on *The Mommies* can still be found
on some channels, many mother characters work,
though it's often part-time, particularly for the married ones, such as Jill (Patricia Richardson) on *Home
Improvement* or Georgie (Patricia Kalember) on *Sisters*. But TV at least addresses the issues with many
women characters who are conflicted about being at
home versus working. Some, like the main character
on *Roseanne* (Roseanne Barr) and Jamie Buchman
(Helen Hunt) on *Mad About You*, are almost brave
dames simply because they have the courage to lead
fuller lives and to take the consequences.

Other semibrave dames, mother division, on
television include the title characters in *Cybill*,
Murphy Brown, and *Grace Under Fire*, as well as
Gloria on *Hope & Gloria*. In the dramas, there is

Dr. Sam Waters on *Profiler* and Dr. Kate Austin on *Chicago Hope*, as well as assistant district attorney Jamie Ross on *Law & Order* and Detective Jill Kirkendall on *NYPD Blue*. Come to think of it, Candice Bergen's Murphy qualifies as a brave dame not because of her celebrated wit and passion for her work, but because, like MTM's Mary Richards, she is a true TV groundbreaker, one of a kind with her political smarts, tough talk, out-of-wedlock baby, and ability to piss off Dan Quayle.

BEING A GOOD MOTHER IN film in the nineties generally means being there for your husband and kids and working, if at all, at something not too taxing. It also can mean being brave—but generally in defense of your brood. These women are passionate about something other than passion, it is true, but they are less than brave dames because what they are protecting is children, home, and hearth. Their courage is presented less as a moral choice than as an instinct.

In the unbelievably jingoistic *Not Without My Daughter* (1991), Betty (Sally Field) does show bravery, but it is for her daughter, Mahtob. Trapped with Mahtob in war-torn Iran, Betty is a victim of an abusive husband who is keeping her in that country against her will. Although he has her under constant surveillance, Betty manages to sneak around Teheran to plot their escape. She learns she could leave without her daughter, but she refuses, sacrificing her own safety for her child's.

In the HBO movie *In the Gloaming* (1997), Glenn Close plays Janet, a repressed WASP mother of a son dying of AIDS. Janet works at a museum but, as she often reminds us, it is as a volunteer—at a place where she feels she is viewed as an aging housewife.

When her son, Dan, comes home, Janet gives up her life, including her volunteer work, to stay home and be with him—and to learn about his life. She acts morally and exhibits bravery in dealing with Dan's illness, though it is a restrained, gentrified bravery. True, Janet's worth is measured strictly in terms of her motherhood. But she is making a sacrifice that seems truly worth making and that is, by definition, temporary. As mothers go, she is one of the class acts.

Gail (Meryl Streep) in *The River Wild* (1994) is a mother who takes her family on a rafting trip that turns dangerous: rough water, bad guys. Though she is defined primarily as a mother (she formerly was a river guide), she, not the father, is the main character in this adventure, guiding her family through the raging white water and facing up to the bad guys. Plus she has terrific muscles. She gets to be the brave one, the active one, although again it's for her children's sake. But it's a thrill to see a superb actress such as Streep rise to meet a physical challenge as well as a moral one.

In *Serial Mom* (1994) we learn that even a female serial killer is defined by home and hearth. The main character in John Waters's satire, Beverly Sutphin (Kathleen Turner), is the quintessential fun mom. Her children love her. Serial Mom bonds with them regularly—she even enjoys watching gory horror flicks with her son, Chip. She also happens to be the suburban housewife run amok, a serial murderer who will literally kill to defend her kids. When her daughter is jilted by her date, Serial Mom whacks him with a fire poker. And when Chip's math teacher tells her Chip isn't doing so well, she promptly gets in her station wagon and runs over him a few times.

Serial Mom is no wimpette; she is physically courageous and cheerful, though obviously sociopathic. She slays one neighbor with a pair of scissors and yet another by dropping an air conditioner on his head. She successfully takes control of her own defense at trial. And a not-guilty verdict doesn't keep her from killing again, mere minutes after it's announced. In the end, though, she is not a brave dame. She is a winsome killer defending her family.

THERE HAS BEEN A RECENT spate of ideal-ized single-mother characters, both in the movies and on television, which started in the late eighties with *Baby Boom* (1987). The ones in film recall *Mildred Pierce*, though now they are often mothers to sons, and those sons, unlike Mildred's cold fish of a daughter, adore their mothers. Also, the moms don't work as hard as Mildred, nor are they as ambitious.

I suppose this is progress, though, in that it shows women capable of managing on their own. There can be no *Father Knows Best* condescension toward the mother when there is no father. Still, these works feature mothers in the traditional roles of nurturer and nose wiper. Not that there's any-thing wrong with that, as the *Seinfeld* crew declared in another context. It would simply be an exhilarating change to see characters who are women of childbearing age get a chance to show what they can do besides be maternal.

In *Jerry Maguire* (1996), for example, Dorothy (Renee Zellweger) is a likable single working mom to a great boy. She claims to be trying to raise a man, not find one (a trademark of any good single mother on screen), but she is panting for her boss, sports agent Jerry Maguire, from the very start. Presumably we're supposed to think Dorothy is a capable, liberated woman. She works, and she even has a male nanny. But the main goal in life for Dorothy—who could pass for a lovesick teenager if she didn't have that little boy—is to get married to a guy who isn't even sure he wants her. (What a contrast to a strong single mother like Ellen Burstyn's Alice in *Alice Doesn't Live Here Anymore* and her TV version in *Alice*, played by Linda Lavin.)

Carol (Helen Hunt) in *As Good as It Gets* (1997) is yet another appealing single working-class mother, a waitress. She has a nice little boy, but a sick one. He's her top priority, but, like Renee Zellweger, she ends up in a relationship with a man. And not just any man—a particularly difficult and bigoted one, though (as played by Jack Nicholson) a charming one. Unfortunately, he's not just her boyfriend but her savior, paying for her son's medical treatment. The message here is that even if you work really hard, you're still going to need a man to bail you out. So while Carol looks and talks like a brave dame, she's really more (I hate to say it—I liked her so much) a near-wimpette.

There is probably no need for even a single word to be written about the movie *Striptease*. But Demi Moore does play another feisty single mom—this time an artist with an older son, Oliver—in *The Juror* (1996), based on a book by George Daces Green. Moore's character, Annie Laird, shares an unusually cheery disposition with her *Striptease* character, at least at the beginning of the film, before the going gets tough. She's also unusual in that she really wants to serve on a jury, even though it will involve placing her son with a baby-sitter for a couple of weeks while she's sequestered.

Once Annie is threatened by a mob representative who insists she vote not guilty, she becomes a weepy, miserable victim and even lashes out at Oliver. She's no wimpette, though, and she has moments of insight and bravery. She's able to figure out that her phones are tapped and—in a performance most litigators would envy—to persuade ten jurors to switch their votes from guilty to not guilty. Later Annie fools government prosecutors and successfully (and unbelievably) takes on the mob by herself. As with most brave moms in the movies, though, she's in a defensive position, acting to save her child.

In the witty and moving Meg Wolitzer novel *This Is Your Life*, Dottie Ingels, a single mother of two girls, is trying to make it as a stand-up comic.

She adores her kids and actually seems to have fun with them, but when her career starts to get going, she grabs the chance and takes off for L.A., leaving them in New York for a few weeks with a slew of her bizarre friends as baby-sitters. She also is not above using her kids' personal lives in her routine.

In the Nora Ephron–directed film adaptation, *This Is My Life*, with Julie Kavner in the starring role, Dottie walks in on her older daughter doing a wicked imitation of her. Dottie laments that she has no one to help her, no one to leave her children with, and asks whether she should be working at a Macy's cosmetic counter forever.

The novel and the film get credit for answering this question with a no—and for taking on the subject of work and motherhood in a compassionate, realistic, and funny way.

A FEW REALLY BRAVE DAMES

It's the rare mother who isn't defined solely as a mother, or a wife and mother. One of the great mother characters comes from the James Cameron pre-*Titanic* action movie *Terminator 2: Judgment Day* (1991). Single mother Sarah Connor (Linda Hamilton) is a worthy successor to Jane Eyre. She is strong, independent, and bold. She's also a whole lot tougher than she was in *The Terminator* (1984).

In the original *Terminator*, Sarah frequently wept and didn't do much without her protector from the future (and father of her child), Kyle Reese. She got to utter lines like, "Come on, do I look like the mother of the future? I mean, am I tough? Organized? I can't even balance my checkbook." She also made some what-can-you-expect-from-a-girl moves, like calling her mother (in fact, Schwarzenegger posing as her mother) when she was on the run and giving her (him) the phone number of her room.

The second time around, Sarah is willing to risk everything for her son, John, and—like a male action hero—for a cause greater than herself or her child: to save the future. She's the rare "good mother" who smokes, swears, and totes a gun, even in front of her son. And she doesn't even have a home and hearth to defend. We find her first in a mental institution, from which she manages to escape against great odds and in large part due to her own ingenuity. She spends the rest of the film on the run.

Sarah is unstable at times. She is afraid of showing emotion to her son for fear it will make him too soft to be the warrior he must become. She almost blows off the head of a man whose work could help the bad guys in the future, with the man's wife and son close by. It's not because she's a woman, though, but because she has the burden of knowing about the thermonuclear future. But she shoulders her burden and is a certified brave dame.

In *Courage Under Fire* (1996), Meg Ryan plays Captain Karen Walden, a single mother who sees a different kind of action. Assigned to the Persian Gulf during the war there, she's a pilot and leader of a squadron of guys who crash their helicopter in enemy territory. She's brave, moral, just, and passionate about her calling. She explains that though it's very difficult, she must leave her daughter behind and fight for her country. And her daughter appears to be well adjusted and adored by her mom.

Captain Walden refuses to leave an injured member of her team so that the rest can try to escape to safety. And, in what turns out to be a fatal decision, she lets her men go ahead when a rescue helicopter shows up nearby, even though she's gravely injured.

Alas, this paragon of women in film spends the entire movie dead (one of her men having told the rescue team she was already a goner as she lay there injured). Karen Walden is seen only in flashback, as a dogged investigator tries to find out what happened in the Gulf so that she can get a posthumous Medal of Honor.

Not only can a dead woman be a brave dame, but a pregnant one can, too. Marge Gunderson (Frances McDormand) in *Fargo* (1996) is one of the finest women characters in film, one of the bravest of the brave dames. She may be big with child, but being seven months pregnant doesn't define her—her work as a police chief and detective does. Marge's disposition is sunny, she's a loving and devoted wife, and she never emits so much as a single whine (in stark contrast to a character like Marisa Tomei's in *The Paper*). Marge doesn't even have the baby before the film ends.

Sure, there are references to the pregnancy, as with Marge's constant hunger and eating, or when she almost vomits from morning sickness (though her nausea comes on the heels of having viewed a murder victim). And she wisely uses her pregnancy to serve her professional interests, as when she visits a suspect who won't invite her to sit ("Mind if I sit down? I'm carrying quite a load here").

But her pregnancy never keeps Marge from being resolute (she spends a lot of time trudging around in the snow hunting down leads), being a good marksman (she shoots a perp in the leg), and generally doing her job well and with a sense of humor.

In Stephen McCauley's delightful, intelligent novel *The Object of My Affection*, the protagonist is George, a gay man. In the 1998 film, the focus is on Nina, the book's second main character (Jennifer Aniston). She does have her baby, but the movie is the rare one to spare us the trite perspiration of labor and the grunts of delivery. Instead, we see Nina begin to have a contraction, and the next shot is of her holding the baby. As with *Fargo, The Object of My Affection* also dispenses with the obligatory beautiful nursery shots and treacly baby shower scenes so often seen in movies featuring pregnant women.

More significant is that Nina and those around her barely discuss her pregnancy. Instead, the movie is about Nina's romantic life, and George's. Will Nina be able to make a life with George, who has agreed to participate in the raising of the child, though their friendship remains platonic? Will she end up with someone else? Will he? Though the baby's father figures in the plot, there is no discussion of marriage or of how she will cope as a single mother. It is just assumed that she will because, clearly, she is a brave dame.

LONG BEFORE *DR. QUINN, MEDICINE Wo-man* came to television, there was *The Big Valley* (1965–69) with Barbara Stanwyck playing Victoria Barkley, the owner, matriarch, and boss of the sprawling Barkley Ranch. She led her four children in fighting off bandits, killers, and con men. Victoria Barkley and Dr. Quinn prove that setting a show or a film in an earlier era doesn't have to be an excuse for keeping a mother at home, as it was with the TV show *The Wonder Years* and the film *The Bridges of Madison County*—and countless others. In fact, Michaela Quinn (Jane Seymour) is brave, strong, kind, and moral—a Jane Eyre from nineties prime-time television living in nineteenth-century America instead of England.

"Dr. Mike" starts out single and childless. She moves by herself from Boston to the frontier town of Colorado Springs in the 1860s after the death of her father and medical partner. She sets up her practice immediately, but it takes time for her to be accepted into the community. Her one immediate friend asks Dr. Mike to adopt her three children as she lies dying from a snakebite. Thus Dr. Mike becomes a single working mother.

Gradually she also becomes a respected member of the community, too. When she isn't healing the sick or caring for her children, she supports

Indian rights, seeks equality for the blacks in Colorado Springs, and sympathizes with the barmaids/prostitutes who work in the local saloon/brothel. And, eventually, she gets the guy—handsome, rugged mountain man Byron Sully. They married at the end of the 1994–95 season, and she got pregnant shortly thereafter.

Unfortunately, after her marriage the show became more soap opera than adventure, and Dr. Mike was seen in her wife-and-mother role far more than in her doctor role, thus making her some hoary TV executive's idea of a good woman, not a regular viewer's idea of a brave dame. Maybe that's why *Dr. Quinn, Medicine Woman* got the ax.

THERE ARE FOUR NOTABLE WOMEN characters, stellar brave dames, who are not mothers, who do not technically belong in this chapter, yet who deserve to be mentioned because they have important relationships with children as surrogate mothers.

Margaret Atwood's brilliant dystopian novel *A Handmaid's Tale* is set in the near future when America is ruled by a right-wing religious dictatorship and women of childbearing age such as the hero, Offred (not allowed her own identity, she is "Of Fred"), are kept for breeding. She is a handmaid, a surrogate mother. When their children are born, handmaids must give them over to the supposedly "morally fit" wives of the theocrats, the so-called Christians who rule.

Offred is a grand creation. Her insurrectionary spirit does not blaze forth overnight, nor is her rebellion a Hollywood makeover into a wild and crazy guerrilla. But she is brave, passionate, and just—a fine successor to Jane Eyre.

On-screen, single, childless women characters are often defined by their relationships with children as well, as though Hollywood can't resist making every women a mother. Reggie Love (Susan Sarandon) in *The Client* (1994) (also a John Grisham book and a television show) is a strong female character, though one with a flawed past. A tough attorney who is also attractive, sympathetic, and single, Reggie loves the law. In the movie and the novel, she spends much of her time as a surrogate mother to her young client, a boy whose own mother, though not a bad one, is poor and unable to help her son get out of trouble. Reggie doesn't save him through tenderness, however; she saves him through her smarts.

In *Smilla's Sense of Snow*, Peter Høeg's fine,

atmospheric novel, Smilla Jaspersen (played by Julia Ormond in the not-very-distinguished film version), half Dane, half Inuit, an expert on ice and snow, acts as surrogate mother to Isaiah, the six-year-old son of a neighboring woman who is poor, uneducated, and a drunk. Smilla plays with him, bathes him, and lets him sleep with her when his apartment is too unruly. When Isaiah mysteriously dies, Smilla smells a rat and takes it upon herself to investigate what she believes was a murder. She is a brave dame, adventurous and passionate about what she is doing, although this passion, too, is initially derived from her relationship with a child. However, her quest ultimately brings her to confront an even greater issue, the ecology of Greenland, and she faces it with consummate courage.

Patrick Dennis's comic novel *Auntie Mame* became a play (written by Jerome Lawrence and Robert E. Lee) and a movie (written by Betty Comden and Adolph Green), both of which starred Rosalind Russell. The plot is set mostly in the twenties and thirties, and Mame Dennis is a wealthy, sophisticated New Yorker who suddenly discovers herself sole guardian of her orphaned nephew, Patrick. She's a social butterfly, a hilarious dilettante, but what comes across in all three versions is not only Mame's unwavering love for this child, but her passion for fairness. A brave dame, she stands up to bigots and bullies with great moral authority—and fabulous clothes.

THE TRUE WIMPETTE IS TERMINALLY self-effacing, so it should come as no surprise that in the misogynistic wimpette world, the best mother is often a father. Think of all those films with great dads and dead or incapacitated mothers: *Sabrina*, *Father's Day*, *The American President*, *Sleepless in Seattle*, *To Gillian on Her 37th Birthday*, *My Father the Hero*, *Three Men and a Baby* and its sequel *Three Men and a Little Lady*, *My Girl*, *The Lion King*, and *Beauty and the Beast*. Dads and surrogate dads are more perfect moms than any genuine woman could ever be—and they usually get to keep their day jobs.

4

Friends and Sisters

And, of Course, Wimpettes and
Brave Dames

Okay, the good news about sisterhood: Movies such as the stylish *Stage Door* (1937), sitcoms like the sweetly silly *My Friend Irma* (1952–54), and books such as Dodie Smith's incandescent coming-of-age novel *I Capture the Castle* (1948) used to be not only few and far between, but overshadowed by a monumental number of works about sisters and women friends featuring catfights, egregious sneakiness, and blatant betrayals. And what were all the battles about? Democracy versus fascism? Please. You know and I know that female characters, no matter how good-natured, educated, or well-bred, were routinely depicted as willing—no, eager—to toss aside their closest female friends or their flesh-and-blood siblings for a guy. It has gotten better. Still, if you look closely, you'll discover that some of those sunny smiles of sisterhood are really bared teeth.

There is also one new wrinkle I want to mention. Many novels, movies, and TV shows that celebrate sisterhood venerate women and denigrate men. Where wimpettes once wrote off half of humanity—their own sex—now they're being shown writing off the other. Too many of the new women-are-wonderful books and films are shamefully anti-men. Guys are depicted as abusive, socially or emotionally obtuse, or merely flatulent louts, although the more politically correct of these works are shrewd enough to concede one good male character. What this revisionist women-are-good, men-are-bad setup leads to is yet one more generation of weak sisters. Their very prejudice reveals what losers they are. Strutting about, flexing meaningless muscles, they exhibit the same condescension and sexism they decry in men. Guys-don't-get-it humor is the nineties equivalent of racist or ethnic jokes.

Nevertheless, misogyny continues to be more widespread then misandry. So when female buddies do appear on-screen—which is still a lot less frequently than male buddies—the women are often pitted against each other, ethical dummkopfs, unable to comprehend the value of friendship.

True, in the sixty-two-year-old movie *Stage Door,* the aristocratic Terry Randall (Katharine Hepburn) does look down her perfectly sculpted nose and pronounce to her roommate, the plebeian Jean Maitland (Ginger Rogers): "I see that in addition to your other charms you have the insolence generated by an inferior upbringing." But there is far more depth in this film than in many current releases with their banal dialogue and cheap catfights. In *Stage Door'*s screenplay, by Morrie Ryskind and Anthony Veiller, based on the Edna Ferber and George S. Kaufman play, there is recognition that relationships between women— between people—are complicated by economic, social, and psychological realities. The triumph of *Stage Door* is its depiction of a querulous theatrical sorority that, ultimately, is able to transcend the barriers of social class, personal morality, and even talent.

WIMPETTES

Women friends and sisters in film, novels, and television not only routinely betray each other, but indulge in cruel gossip, mocking the very idea of intimacy. (What else is "cattiness" but a comparison to an animal, a denial of full humanity?) In fiction, the women's friendship genre—those sagas of four or five friends who meet in school or on the job—routinely features some act of female faithlessness. (Terry McMillan's *Waiting to Exhale* is a bright and witty exception.) Remember the film *The Women* (1939), from Clare Booth's play? Marvelously arch and deliciously camp, in its day it was publicized as "135 women with men on their minds!" I admit it's still a hoot to watch, but not one of those 135 had real courage. *The Women*'s women are vain, vapid, self-effacing to the point of masochism, materialistic, or downright treacherous. That female-versus-female tradition continues today in films such as *Heathers*, *Soapdish*, *My Best Friend's Wedding*, and *Hope Floats*, and on TV shows such as *Dallas*, *Dynasty*, and *Melrose Place*. Jane Austen's world of courteous women—loving to each other, or at least civil—seems a century or two in the future rather than a part of our past.

Hope Floats (1998), a sinker on many levels, is typical. Birdee Pruitt (Sandra Bullock) appears on a talk show on national television for—she thinks—a makeover. What the on-screen television (and also the film's) audience already knows when she makes her entrance is that her best friend has lured her there under false pretenses in order to humiliate her in front of the world—by announcing that she and Birdee's husband have been having a torrid affair. It's painful to see the bright, with-it actress of *A Time to Kill* and *The Net* play such a wimpette.

Julia Roberts, the star who seemed so strong in *Mystic Pizza* and *The Pelican Brief*, plays one of two wimpettes in 1997's *My Best Friend's Wedding*. Food critic Julianne Potter, instead of decrying the national surfeit of coriander, is obsessed with getting married. She does everything in her power to sabotage the wedding of her best friend, Michael, to upper-class, stunning Kimmy. Although Julianne and Kimmy have never met until Michael introduces them four days before the wedding, Kimmy, the other wimpette (played by Cameron Diaz), believes she's found a new best friend—a clue to her character's emotional depth, to say nothing of her IQ. And Julianne pretends she too has met her female soul mate in order to achieve her nefarious goal, a clear illustration of Article Six of wimpette philosophy, that a woman betrays other women, including her friends. (And while we're at it, Article Three applies as well, that a wimpette always opts for indirection and subterfuge.)

Julianne spends the rest of the movie betraying her friendship with Michael—so that she might marry him. And all during these machinations, she pretends to reciprocate Kimmy's affection while extracting information to use against her. In the final act, Julianne and Kimmy engage in the requisite catfight in a ladies' room. Someone even shouts, "Catfight!" presumably so that the "chick flick" audience will comprehend what's going on. The other women in the room gather around to cheer Kimmy and yell "bitch" and "tramp" at Julianne.

The best friend gone bad is a popular suspense thriller theme as well, as if there is a universal fear that all female friendships are tainted by perfidy. In these films, a sympathetic wimpette is typically the victim of a conniving—and potentially lethal— "friend," a strong woman in the mold of Anjelica Huston's character in *The Grifters*. In *Poison Ivy* (1992), poor student Ivy, played by Drew Barrymore, pretends to be best friend to rich Cooper (Sara Gilbert) and ends up living with Cooper's family. (We know Cooper is rich because her first name is a last name.) When Ivy meets Cooper's dad for the first time, Cooper lets herself be relegated to the backseat and sits there as her friend proceeds to flash the old man some thigh. Once Ivy is in residence, she preys on Cooper's whole family, ultimately seducing Cooper's father and killing off her ailing mother. She even co-opts the family dog. Ultimately Ivy, like Julianne in *My Best Friend's Wedding*, is punished—in her case with death. As with most of the alleged heroines in this genre, Cooper is gullible and vulnerable—a true wimpette.

In *Diabolique* (1996), a flabby remake of the taut *Les Diaboliques* (1954), another film with a female friend as devil woman, Nicole (Sharon Stone) pretends to plot with her best friend, Mia (Isabelle Adjani)—who the film hints is also her lover—to kill Mia's husband, Guy, a sadist who has also been sleeping with Nicole. In fact, Nicole and Guy (heh, heh) have been plotting to get rid of Mia. Mia is a double-whammy wimpette, a two-time victim, morally and physically weak. She suffers from a heart problem and stays with an abusive sicko of a husband even after finding out he was sleeping with her best friend.

Allison (Bridget Fonda) in *Single White Female* (1992) is the wimpette victim of her evil roommate, Hedra (Jennifer Jason Leigh), whom she meets through an ad. During the course of the film, Allie remains mum and totally gullible as Hedra usurps her look—from her hairstyle to her clothes—seduces her boyfriend, and generally sabotages her life. Here again the strong woman is a demon, the wimpette a hero.

WOMEN WHO BETRAY OR ARE betrayed aren't the only kinds of wimpettes among friends. There are also the women who get side-tracked by love—in a way that male buddies in movies and on television never do.

In *Steel Magnolias* (1989), only one of the characters, Clairee (Olympia Dukakis), doesn't lose her heart and good sense over a man and behave like an utter wimpette. Shelby (Julia Roberts) risks her life getting pregnant to please a husband, Truvy (Dolly Parton) exhausts herself bucking up a good-looking freeloader with the personality of mayonnaise, and Ouiser (Shirley MacLaine) relinquishes her fierce independence by keeping company with a gent who has the appearance and intellect of a Smurf.

In *Waiting to Exhale* (1995), based on the Terry McMillan best-seller, as in *Steel Magnolias*, four women looking for love and happiness console and confide in each other. The film has several "you go, girl" female-bonding scenes, and the women do not betray each other. But for all their liveliness and intelligence, these women are still wimpettes in that they are reacting to men. They spend most of their time either talking about them or weeping over them. And three of them— Savannah (Whitney Houston), Bernadine (Angela Bassett), and Robin (Lela Rochon)—give the impression that if the right man or even the wrong one came along, they'd have no need for their lady friends.

Only Gloria (Loretta Devine), a single mother of a teenage son, the plainest and most sensible of the four (she scolds Bernadine for being "stupid and childish" when she tries to call her ex-husband's new girlfriend after a few drinks), comes across like Clairee in *Steel Magnolias*—as having the backbone to remain a good friend to the others even if a man comes along.

With women buddies, the power of the friendship is diminished by the energy expended on men. No such impediments are permitted in male buddy films and TV shows. Women are often absent entirely, or are little more than set decoration. Or they are used as a device to show that, despite the intensity of a friendship, the guys are unequivocally heterosexual. No matter how beguiling the female—Minnie Driver in *Good Will Hunting*, Linda Fiorentino in *Men in Black*, Maxine Bahns in *The Brothers McMullen*, Julianna Margulies in *The Newton Boys*—she never truly breaks the male bond, much less gets to be the friend herself.

In all types of male buddy films—somber ones like *All the President's Men* and *Midnight Cowboy*, or sunny ones like *48 Hours, The Road to Morocco, City Slickers*, and the four *Lethal Weapon* movies—

there is never any doubt that the most important value is friendship. The audience knows in its collective heart that Bob Hope, Billy Crystal, and Danny Glover would never wimp out; they would die for a friend. (The 1997 film *Inventing the Abbotts* is the rare exception in which a brother betrays a brother for a woman.)

I N TOO MANY MOVIES ABOUT friends and sisters, there are characters who illustrate Article Four of the wimpette philosophy: Men are strong and women are weak. Not only are women portrayed as airheaded, they're lead-assed as well. They are habitually shown as something less than fully alive. Woman friends and sisters don't walk tall. Instead, they literally sit around as though tethered, talking about men or "women's topics": hot flashes, children, glass ceilings. When they do move, they jog, do sit-ups, or walk on a treadmill sweating pretty Hollywood sweat, going nowhere. Women buddies rarely get to be brave. At their best, they're merely assertive. There is little motion in the motion picture.

The women in *Steel Magnolias*, for example, excel at sitting—except when influenced by events beyond their control. They sit around Truvy's Beauty Spot getting back-combed, dyed, lip-waxed, and manicured—and they talk. When there is action in these films, however, it is traditionally female action: sewing (as in *How to Make an American Quilt*) or cooking. The title character played by Mare Winningham in *Georgia* (1995) cooks, as do Idgie and Ruth in *Fried Green Tomatoes*, the aunties in *The Joy Luck Club* (1993), and Shelby and Percy in *The Spitfire Grill* (1996). Now, sewing and cooking can be both creative and constructive, but they are repetitive exercises in which the challenge is internal—in the head, indoors. Specifically, they are about home and hearth, not about being engaged in the world. They are rarely meant to electrify; they are meant to soothe.

Forget mere inertia: Many of the women who are female buddies and sisters are often victims of life-threatening illnesses, such as Beth in *Little Women*, requiring them to lie supine for some part of the film. Other films in which you see this are *Marvin's Room* (1996), *Fried Green Tomatoes*, *Steel Magnolias*, *Beaches* (1988), and *Diabolique* (1996).

While a male buddy may have a disability— like Dustin Hoffman's character's autism in *Rain Man,* the blindness of Al Pacino's colonel in *Scent of a Woman*, or David Strathairn's computer hacker in *Sneakers*—guys are hardly ever faced with life-threatening illness. Their disabilities rarely relegate them to bed, as they almost always do with women. Al Pacino's character may be blind, but he can still drive a Ferrari and dance a tango to die for. The blind hacker in *Sneakers* drives a van to rescue Robert Redford's character.[7] When a male buddy does get laid up, it's usually for a good reason, such as being injured in combat—not because he has randomly been stricken by disease.

In *Thelma and Louise* (1991), two women finally do get off their duffs, just like in a male buddy movie. They even sweat. The only problem is that this film is about as far from the "feminist statement" it was touted to be as a film can get. Thelma (Geena Davis) and Louise (Susan Sarandon) are still reacting to men. When men— Thelma's husband and then a rapist—anger them, they react not as crafty avengers but as typical "emotional" women. Their revenge is neither intelligent nor focused. Those two could not think their way out of a paper bag. (Naturally, they are punished for their adventure—they go over the

7. For more on the difference between the way blind men and women are portrayed on-screen, see Michele Wilens, "Hollywood Isn't Blind to the Possibilities . . . for Men," *The New York Times,* Jan. 24, 1994, p. 23.

edge of a cliff in freeze frame, as if the Hays Code were still in effect.) They illustrate Article Seven, that wimpettes blame their lack of action on others, in this case men.

As soon as Thelma and Louise hit the road, Thelma gets drunk at a bar and starts flirting with a man, annoying Louise. The first significant act of this buddy film is this man's attempted rape of Thelma, and Louise's overblown reaction to it; she gets out her gun and shoots him. This act and Louise's own earlier rape in Texas—which is hinted at but not confirmed until the end of the film—is what binds the two women together.

Their shared victimhood doesn't even bring them together at first. Instead, when they stop at a diner they bicker, in a scene more reminiscent of the farcical male-buddies-on-the-run played by Steve Buscemi and Peter Stormare in *Fargo* than Paul Newman and Robert Redford in *Butch Cassidy and the Sundance Kid* or any other true "guy's guys."

Though neither of these women is long on rationality, Louise is the more sensible. She announces repeatedly that she is going to figure out what to do before getting around to figuring anything out, but at least she is interested in figuring. In contrast, Thelma is the greater wimpette. She takes no responsibility for their situation initially and cries a lot.

The two women quarrel again when J.D. (Brad Pitt) enters the scene. Again Louise acts sensibly, recognizing that giving this fellow a ride would be inadvisable. But J.D. figuratively knocks what little sense there was in Thelma right out of her. She trusts him implicitly, even though he admits he is an armed robber. Although she and Louise are on the lam, Thelma allows J.D. to take her picture and lets slip to him that they are heading to Mexico. Goofy from the great sex she ends up having with him, she leaves this admitted criminal in her motel room with all of their money, which he of course steals.

After Thelma—as Louise puts it—finally "gets laid properly," she starts taking charge. Unfortunately, this involves one impulsive, emotional response after another. She goes on a one-woman crime spree, which she begins (without discussing it first with Louise, who is waiting in the car) by robbing a convenience store at gunpoint while being videotaped by a surveillance camera. Soon thereafter they're pulled over, and Thelma pulls a gun on the cop, again acting on impulse. (A word about "gets laid properly." What a stunningly condescending remedy to proffer. Good sex can indeed put a smile on the face and/or a song in the heart. But how does getting laid make a woman a better person? Have you ever read a

novel or seen a film in which a man's having satis-
fying sex transformed his life or improved his
character?)

Thelma and Louise commit their final, melo-
dramatic acts as a pair. First they react to a leering
truck driver by blowing up his truck. Then, once
the police surround them, they drive off that cliff.
They cannot take control of their lives, so they
simply just escape them. They are not brave
dames. They are wimpettes. Good riddance.

NEAR-WIMPETTES AND
SEMIBRAVE DAMES

A FEW FILMS—SOME GOOD, SOME unspeak-
ably dreadful—portray women buddies or
sisters in a favorable light. They do not betray each
other. Yet these women don't ascend to brave
dame status because their courage is not the over-
riding value of the movie. The three main characters in *The Lemon Sisters* (1990)—Frankie (Carol
Kane), Eloise (Diane Keaton), and Nola (Kathryn
Grody)—are a tightly knit group of girlfriends
who have known each other since childhood.
These friends help each other when one is sick or
needs money, and though men are around, they
don't get in the way. Abby (Janeane Garofalo) and

Noelle (Uma Thurman) in *The Truth About Cats and Dogs* (1996) are friends who support each other in a Cyrano-like scheme to attract a man to Abby. In *Now and Then* (1995), Roberta (Rosie O'Donnell), Sam (Demi Moore), Chrissie (Rita Wilson), and Tina (Melanie Griffith) are also close friends since childhood who, though their lives have gone in different directions, are still good to each other.

In *Moonlight and Valentino* (1995), newly widowed Rebecca (Elizabeth Perkins) bonds with her sister, Lucy (Gwyneth Paltrow), best friend, Sylvie (Whoopi Goldberg), and stepmother, Alberta (Kathleen Turner). Becky (Rosie O'Donnell) is a true-blue pal to lovelorn Annie (Meg Ryan) in *Sleepless in Seattle* (1993). Even the soft-porn *Showgirls* (1995) depicts its main character, Nomi (Elizabeth Berkley), as a devoted friend. In *Something to Talk About* (1995), sisters Grace (Julia Roberts) and Emma Rae (Kyra Sedgwick) understand what loyalty means. Laurel (Bonnie Hunt) is a similar wisecracking but supportive sister to wimpette Dorothy (Renee Zellweger) in *Jerry Maguire*.

The recent remakes of classic novels such as *Sense and Sensibility*, *Emma* (and its modern version, *Clueless*), *Howard's End*, *Little Women*, and *Pride and Prejudice*, as well as *Enchanted April* (from a work by Elizabeth von Arnim), have provided additional admirable sisters and friends on the screen. Of course, there's no shortage of conniving women posing as friends in the remakes of the classics, either, as in *A Portrait of a Lady* and *Wings of the Dove*.

THERE ARE SOME NOTABLE EXCEPTIONS to all the sitting around, where women are allowed to take action or go on an adventure. *Thelma and Louise* is in this category, and women also hit the road in *A League of Their Own, Manny and Lo,* and *Romy and Michele's High School Reunion.* In *Boys on the Side* (1995), Jane (Whoopi Goldberg) decides to head out west in search of her destiny and picks up two other women (Mary-Louise Parker and Drew Barrymore) along the way. This potentially affecting film is weakened rather than strengthened by having the Parker character succumb to yet another affliction, this time AIDS. Another dead dame.

In *The First Wives Club* (1996), based on Olivia Goldsmith's novel, the three main characters— old college chums Elise (Goldie Hawn), Brenda (Bette Midler), and Annie (Diane Keaton)—get to have an escapade. But again, it's all about men. Instead of being sidetracked by love, these women—like Thelma and Louise—are reacting to men they hate.

And it's not just men they hate. They're vicious, albeit funny, about everyone, including younger women ("Pop Tarts" and "infants"), and even about each other when they meet up again many years after college. When asked whether Elise has had any plastic surgery, Brenda quips she's "a quilt."

Their attitudes toward each other change as soon as they devise their plan—to wreak havoc in the lives of the ex-husbands who wronged them. They have their bonding moments, but there's also a boozed-up scene where they doubt and scorn each other. They are together for one reason only: revenge on their exes. If that reason ceased to be, they might quickly become overt wimpettes, back to calling each other names.

Best friends Romy (Mira Sorvino) and Michele (Lisa Kudrow) take a road trip to their reunion in *Romy and Michele's High School Reunion* (1997). In many ways these two might seem stereotypical wimpettes—they're materialistic and sometimes shallow, congenital flakes. Yet during the course of this comedy they show unexpected smarts, overcome their self-doubts left over from high school, and end up happy with the perfect jobs in their very own boutique. All the while they're on an adventure. They're not victims, and they never once betray each other. (In fact, their biggest disagreement is over who is a bigger success "cuteness-wise.") Still, they don't quite qualify as brave dames. They have no real ethical code beyond their loyalty to each other and, quite frankly, they're simply too unremittingly ditzy to be taken seriously as great comic characters, as were Judy Holliday in *Born Yesterday* and Carole Lombard in *Mr. and Mrs. Smith*.

Manny and Lo (1996) are foster children whose addict mother has died. The two sisters hide out in empty "model homes" and vacation houses while Lo is pregnant. They are the opposite of homebound—they don't even have a home. They're on the road, at large, and on a unique adventure. They have their share of sisterly arguments, and Lo is clearly and realistically annoyed with her younger sibling most of the time. They are true to each other, but their kidnapping, squatting in people's houses, and shoplifting shows they are something less than scrupulously moral.

Outside the realm of campy television characters such as Alexis (Joan Collins) on *Dynasty* and *Melrose Place*'s Amanda (Heather Locklear in the early seasons), Kimberly (Marcia Cross), Sydney (Laura Leighton), and Brooke (Kristin Davis), television provides a number of realistic female friends and sisters who don't wimp out on each other.

On *Cybill,* an Americanized *Absolutely Fabulous*, actress Cybill (Cybill Shepherd) and her rich, boozy best friend, Maryann (Christine Baranski), lunch together, dish together, and never stab each other in the back. They confront menopause as one, ingesting herbs by the dozen and discussing why they really don't need plastic surgery. There is, alas, some tiresome rivalry, though not between these two; when Maryann's ex, Dr. Dick, marries the surgically enhanced Morgan Fairchild, Cybill puts the new wife in her place in a food fight reminiscent of the Krystle and Alexis knock-down-drag-out in the reflecting pool on *Dynasty*. Their friendship is fun to watch, but like many of their sisters on TV, they are not facing extraordinary circumstances that might put their loyalty and courage to the test.

Though buttoned-down, ever-optimistic TV producer Hope (Cynthia Stevenson) and flashy, outspoken hairdresser Gloria (Jessica Lundy) on

Hope & Gloria appear to have little in common, the two neighbors become fast friends. They do quarrel—as when Hope hates her computer dating service date but likes Gloria's, or when Gloria agrees to paint Hope's apartment but can't get it done. Yet they always quickly reconcile. There's never any backstabbing between these lively women.

Roseanne and Jackie (Laurie Metcalf), her cop-turned-truck-driver sister on *Roseanne*, often bicker and even disagree about larger issues, but they never double-cross each other. Jackie is a constant presence in the Conner household and is involved with Roseanne's three kids. When Becky goes to the gynecologist for the first time, Roseanne and Jackie are more nervous than she is. And when Jackie is pregnant, Roseanne is a supportive sister. She is not quite a brave dame because of her everydayness, but no wimpette could survive in the Conner household.

As for *Sisters*, the Reed women—Alex (Swoosie Kurtz), Teddy (Sela Ward), Georgie (Patricia Kalember), and Frankie (Julianne Phillips)—on the well-acted prime-time soap opera are generally decent to each other. They come together to help their mother, Bea, after their father dies. Georgie even carries a child for Frankie, who is unable to conceive. At other times, though, they descend to typical soap opera wimpette tactics, behaving with treachery and bitchery. Teddy, the most unstable of the four, tries to win her ex, Mitch, away from Frankie when Frankie is dating him, and then invades their wedding with a shotgun.

Other friends on nineties TV who hark back to the warmth of Lucy and Ethel on *I Love Lucy*— as well as the title characters in shows such as *Cagney & Lacey*, *Kate and Allie*, *The Golden Girls*, and *Designing Women*—include brave dame Xena and pal Gabrielle on *Xena: Warrior Princess*, brave dame Buffy and Willow on *Buffy the Vampire Slayer*, and brave dame Dr. Mike and Charlotte on *Dr. Quinn, Medicine Woman*. Also there are Jamie and Fran on *Mad About You*, Grace and Nadine in *Grace Under Fire*, Susan and Vicki on *Suddenly Susan*, Annie and Caroline on *Caroline in the City*, and Ally and Angel on *Profiler*, where Angel also serves as baby-sitter, a true sign of a loving friend to a single mom.

BRAVE DAME FRIENDS AND SISTERS

Betrayal among women in movies is so common that at first glance *All About Eve* (1950) seems merely the wittiest and most sophisticated example of the genre. But although young Eve Harrington

(Anne Baxter) does deal treacherously with her older mentor, the great Broadway star Margo Channing (Bette Davis), the subplot tells a finer story. Karen Richards (Celeste Holm) is Margo's friend, and while she does have a moment of weakness and allows the wildly ambitious Eve to get her nasty foot in the door, she quickly regrets her action and makes up for it. The friendship between the world-famous actress and the house-wife is a fascinating and rewarding one because of these two brave dames' humor, charm, and love for each other.

There are also some more recent notable exceptions to the backstabbing buddies stereo-types, in the mold of movies such as *Julia*, in which the Lillian Hellman character (Jane Fonda) is portrayed as willing to risk her life for her friend, the valiant Julia (Vanessa Redgrave), a hero and martyr. In *Beaches* and *Mystic Pizza* (as well as in Wendy Wasserstein's play *The Sisters Rosenzweig*, a mature and witty contemplation of sororal rela-tions in an upper-middle-class family), women wind up being true. And those two street-smart cops on TV's *Cagney & Lacey* were brave dames whose lives depended on each other.

Though they have their share of arguments, the baseball players in *A League of Their Own* (1992) understand teamwork—and friendship. When one of the women trying out for the team can't find her name on a list of who made the cut because she can't read, another comes to help her—and all of the women on the field applaud when she does find her name. Also, these women are not merely active but athletic, some of the few since *Personal Best*. They play baseball, and they're on the road, though they also go to finishing school. In a nice twist, their manager, Jimmy Dugan (Tom Hanks), is the one sitting around most of the time, while the women are in motion. They are brave dames, on and off the field.

THESE DAYS, WOMEN VALUING OTHER women is a socially correct attitude that indicates political maturity and a healthy self-image. It's swell for girlfriends and sisters, but potentially problematic for artists. When a notion about relationships becomes not just au courant but is seen as a virtue, it is difficult to write about that relationship truthfully and unself-consciously.

Emotional truth does not proceed from an ideal, however, no matter how noble that ideal is. My guess is that our portrayals of sisterhood in art will be increasingly honest as we become less attached to the idea of rightness in the relationship and simply live it—as we come to believe it not just in our heads but in our guts. What tale of friendship today has the simple power of the biblical tale of Ruth and Naomi? How many sister movies can beat D. W. Griffith's silent *Orphans of the Storm* (1921)? Those were far from the good old days for women. But those stories are still moving because of their unself-conscious naturalness, their truth. We, alas, have become wimpette-inured. We have witnessed so many dying heroes, from *La Bohème's* Mimi to Rose of *A Thousand Acres*, so many catfights, and so much bitchery that we still have trouble summoning up that simple love.

5

Single Women . . . All the Rest

BEING SINGLE . . . IT CAN DRIVE a girl crazy.
Because if she defies (or is denied) her hor-
monal destiny, which is to be wife and mother,
she becomes an unnatural female *thing*. Remember Glenn Close's psychotic Alex in *Fatal Attraction*? Not only does she look like a Gorgon—albeit
a sexy blond one—she also acts like some hideous
creature, stalking an upright American family. She
torments her one-night stand, pours acid on his
car, cooks his little girl's bunny rabbit, then kid-
naps the child.

After nutsy Alex came other voracious career
women only slightly less appalling: novelist Cather-
ine Trammell (Sharon Stone) in *Basic Instinct* (1992),
computer executive Meredith Johnson (Demi

Moore) in *Disclosure* (1994), and prosecutor Carolyn Polhemus (Greta Scacchi) in *Presumed Innocent* (1990).[8] They were so greedy for sex, so
uninhibited, that they seemed bestial. The message
to men was: Stick to your lukewarm wife. Hot
sex with a free woman is perilous. The message
to everyone was: Bad things happen to strong
women.

Sometimes single professional females on-
screen weren't wild, but they still weren't normal.
If not too hot, they were too cold. Frigid. Or just
old-fashioned, old-maid bitter. Even today,
women characters who refuse to play by neowim-
pette rules, that is, who do not dilute the strength
of their ambition with girlish effervescence, are
not often portrayed as brave dames. Check out
mergers and acquisitions whiz Katharine Parker
(Sigourney Weaver) in *Working Girl* (1988), newspaper editor Alicia Clark (Glenn Close) in *The
Paper* (1994), prosecutor Janet Venable (Laura
Linney) in *Primal Fear* (1996), or TV news anchor
Marcia McGrath (Stockard Channing) in *Up Close
and Personal* (1996). All are hard as nails, cold as

8. For more on these kinds of characters, see Janet Maslin, "Sex and
   Terror: The Male View of the She-Boss," *The New York Times*,
   Jan. 14, 1994, p. C14.

ice, and—the worst calamity in the wimpette universe—unlovable.

WIMPETTES

I find it amazing that even when they have a female protagonist, so many movies begrudge their women heroes their heroism. These main characters aren't valorous; they're defective. I'm not talking about ordinary sins and imperfections that would give them their uniqueness: In *The Wizard of Oz,* Dorothy isn't only brave; she's also homesick and fearful. In other words, she's human.

But instead of normal ambivalence and sensitivity, which is what Dorothy has, what we've been seeing lately in main characters is some crippling vulnerability that sends a subliminal signal to the audience: Relax. She's flawed. She's a *real* woman.

Which brings us to Sigourney Weaver's character, Helen Hudson, in *Copycat* (1995). An expert on serial killers, Hudson is felled by agoraphobia after she is attacked by one of these loonies. Would a male hero in this sort of movie have been so afflicted? Not on your life. He would have taken a slug of hooch and faced his demons. Hudson, on the other hand, hasn't left her apartment in thirteen months. She can barely open the door to get her newspaper. A smart dame? Yes. A brave dame? Not on your life. (*Copycat* is also downright disgraceful in portraying the serial killer's violence against women, which is more sexually explicit than some of what is deemed pornography.)

In *Outbreak*, released the same year as *Copycat* (clearly not filmdom's Year of the Woman), Rene Russo plays Dr. Robby Keough, an expert in disease-causing microorganisms. She is in the throes of a divorce from one of her colleagues, played by Dustin Hoffman. They end up working on the same project involving an outbreak of the deadly Ebola virus. As the film begins, they are equals, but guess which one of them gets nipped by the bug? And although Russo looks as if she could bench-press three Hoffmans, she winds up being not the brave dame she seems to have been set up to be, but the wimpette who lies in bed oozing from a couple of orifices while he gets to ride in a helicopter and save humanity.

In *Conspiracy Theory* (1997), Alice Sutton (Julia Roberts) is a government lawyer who indulges a crazed conspiracy theorist, Jerry Fletcher (Mel Gibson), after he helps her when she's the victim of a mugging. She allows him to visit her at her office—even though he's a raging paranoiac.

Jerry's idiot theories of course turn out to be true, and Alice spends the rest of the film reacting to him and doing what he tells her. Yes, she's portrayed as a single lawyer not dependent on a man. And true, she does get to save Jerry's life while he's in the hospital, although only after, at his direction, she switches charts so that his roommate can be killed instead. But it's a rare moment when Alice isn't following Jerry's orders and looking frightened, and big eyes and quivering lips do not brave dames make.

This is what gets me: Lawyers, such as Alice in *Conspiracy Theory*, are trained to understand how the system works. Yet time and time again, women attorneys are portrayed as being as artless as the proverbial farmer's daughter. What this blatant susceptibility says is that no matter how smart, educated, and sophisticated a woman is, she's still a creature of her emotions. She cannot cut it out in the world. In *Guilty as Sin* (1993), for instance, Jennifer Haines (Rebecca De Mornay) is an ambitious criminal defense lawyer who truly gets off on her work. "Is there anything better than winning?" she demands of her boyfriend when she's fresh from a big courtroom victory. She then—as apparently is the custom of career women nowadays, according to the movies— strips and is ready for office sex before he knows what hit him. Jennifer spends the rest of the film in conservative, if tight-fitting, coat-dresses and suits that presumably signal she's a serious person and has more than just lust on the brain. She does seem a powerful presence, good at what she does, and definitely not dependent on a man.

Still, it matters not at all that she has studied the law since she was a tyke and can win a big case. Jennifer ends up a victim, à la Glenn Close's barrister, Teddy Barnes, in *Jagged Edge* (1985), the prey of her slick, handsome client. Another fool for love. Another wimpette.

Lieutenant Major Joanne Galloway (Demi Moore), a navy lawyer in *A Few Good Men* (1992), is another character who looks like she can cope. Forget about it. She and a less experienced litigator, Danny (Tom Cruise), are appointed to defend two marines implicated in a murder. Danny turns out to be a courtroom crackerjack, no matter that he's just a year out of law school. Joanne ends up as his assistant, even though he was supposed to be working for her. After some initial sparring, she settles happily into her second-string role. "Are you drunk?" she asks him one night when he's clearly stinko. "I'll put on a pot of coffee. We've got a long night's work ahead." When she's not getting Danny coffee during late-night strategy sessions, she's his cheer-leader, flattering him wildly with lines like, "I think you're an exceptional lawyer."

It's not only lawyers who get turned into wimpettes. It's other professionals as well. In *Up Close and Personal* (1996), Michelle Pfeiffer plays Tally Atwater, reporter protégé of veteran TV newsman Warren Justice (Robert Redford). The film leaves the impression that Tally never could have made it without Warren. He is not her mentor, advising her; he is Pygmalion, creating her. He teaches her not only about broadcast news, but also about fashion. He actually accompanies her to a clothing store to pick out the right pastel dresses for her wardrobe, and he consults on her hair and makeup.

Even one of my favorite brave dames, Jane Craig (played by Holly Hunter) in *Broadcast News* (1987), is given a cutesy, girly flaw. When the stress of her job as TV news producer gets to her, she has herself such a good cry that the audience can almost hear the filmmaker's soothing voice: There, there, sweetheart, let it all come out. It's not that stouthearted men and women don't break down on occasion; it's that this big boo-hoo is so jarring, so unoriginal, and so cheap in a film of such vitality.

In *City of Angels* (1998), Meg Ryan is Maggie

Rice, a tough cardiothoracic surgeon who quickly degenerates into a wimpette in a scrub suit, over-reacting to the loss of a patient. By the end of the movie, she has essentially given up her career to keep company with the angel she's fallen for. Actually, by the very end, she's a goner after a truck runs her over, although I suspect that is intended to be a happy moment, as she now can be a real (albeit dead) woman, i.e., a woman with a man.

THERE IS A NEW TENDENCY in wimpette-dom lately. Rather than having a main character who merely does stupid female tricks, have one who is plain stupid. Put a woman in the CEO's chair, give her a prestigious profession, then let her act like a dumb broad. The need to present high-powered women as idiots is apparently irresistible. The two most prominent looks-like-a-brave-dame-but-sure-as-hell-isn't wimpettes on TV today are Veronica "Ronnie" Chase (Kirstie Alley) on *Veronica's Closet* and the title character on the runaway hit *Ally McBeal*, played by Calista Flockhart.

Both series make it clear that if you are a likable single woman, successful in your work, you must behave like an ass and your personal life must be a hideous shambles. If you're strong, you must be insecure. If you're financially independent, you've got to be a neurotic (but adorable) mess. Remember Arnie Becker (Corbin Bernsen) on *L.A. Law*? He had a disastrous personal life and wouldn't win any canon-of-ethics contest, but he was far more professional than these two beauts.

Ronnie is the fortyish owner of Veronica's Closet, a thriving Victoria's Secret–type corporation and purveyor of lingerie and books. How it's flourishing is a mystery, as Ronnie forever seems to be letting her personal problems get in the way of her work and often reacts hysterically and impulsively to her colleagues.

It's hard to figure how those colleagues can take her seriously in the dark velvet loungewear she sports at work, which makes her look as though she belongs on a broom rather than in a boardroom. It's also difficult to conceive how they can take her at all. "Comfort me, comfort me," she demands in her hoarse, breathy voice, and her minions have to come running—that is, when they're not doing ugly little favors for her, like hiding her dog or lying to her ex-husband.

Ronnie spends an inordinate amount of office time worrying about her body and how said

body—actually a perfectly nice, voluptuous one—
is portrayed. When the company is doing a new
catalog, Ronnie spends much of the episode going
gaga over the fact that a body double has been
chosen to replace her figure.

When she isn't obsessing about her body
image, she's preoccupied with weighty issues such
as why her dog likes her ex's new girlfriend better
than her. Yes, this is a sitcom, and it would not
be entertaining to hear Ronnie discuss P&L—
although she does get to say "ASAP" in one episode. But does she have to carry on more about
her own bottom line than the company's?

Like Ronnie, Ally McBeal is miraculously
successful—in her case as a defense lawyer. It's a
rare trial the hapless, neurotic, tremulous, girlish,
moody, coy Ally doesn't win. The most amusing
conceit of this show is not the Dancing Baby, but
that Ally went to Harvard Law School. Harvard
should sue for slander. Ally is forever opening her
mouth without thinking. She also stammers and
wimpettishly says no when she means yes and yes
when she means no. Instead of rolling up her
sleeves and rolling with the punches, she whines
and eats ice cream. The show's considerable charm
and originality are outweighed by dumb-ass lines
like "Whenever I get depressed, I raise my hem-
lines." Untrue, as she gets depressed so often that

by now we would be seeing her pubis, if not her navel.

Ally's success comes despite unprofessional behavior that could get a real-life attorney disbarred. She has no compunction about dating clients, her boss, opposing counsel, and an opposing party. She gets arrested for shoplifting and assault. (This does get her hauled before the state review board, but—as always—she wins.) She squeezes a client's rear end and flirts with the judge on one of her cases in hopes of getting him to rule in her client's favor.

Her first week on the job, Ally informs her boss that she doesn't want to meet with an important prospective client because conference rooms make her feel small and juvenile. Ally is then shown, in one of the show's many camera gimmicks revealing her thoughts, as a Lilliputian figure in an enormous conference room chair. In another episode, she's asked to go to criminal court. "I can't go to criminal court," she wails. "I'm afraid of criminals."

Compare this teeny weenie to other divine lawyers in comedies, Amanda (Katharine Hepburn) in *Adam's Rib* or Glenda (Goldie Hawn) in *Seems Like Old Times*. Or, on a more serious note, to a jurist like Sonny Klonsky in Scott Turow's novel *The Laws of Our Fathers*. Klonsky is smart and appealing and, though she has a romance, she's not fantasizing about ripping her robe off at all hours of the day.

SEMIBRAVE DAMES AND NEAR-WIMPETTES

The next best thing to a brave dame who is successful on her own is one who is paired up with a man with whom she keeps up—or even bests. Though their dialogue does not match the witty repartee of Tracy and Hepburn films, a number of contemporary movies are harking back to egalitarian partnerships of the thirties and forties, with some intelligent back-and-forth between the sexes. I think it began again in the late eighties with *The Big Easy* (1987), with Ellen Barkin and Dennis Quaid, and *When Harry Met Sally . . .* (1989), with Billy Crystal and Meg Ryan. We're seeing more of it lately in movies such as *Speechless* (1994) (Geena Davis and Michael Keaton), *He Said, She Said* (1991) (Elizabeth Perkins and Kevin Bacon), *Tin Cup* (1996) (Rene Russo and Kevin Costner), *Four Weddings and a Funeral* (1994) (Andie MacDowell and Hugh Grant), *One Fine Day* (1996) (Michelle Pfeiffer and George

Clooney), and *I Love Trouble* (1994) (Julia Roberts and Nick Nolte).

On TV, the most original partner/pal is *Seinfeld*'s Elaine Benes (Julia Louis-Dreyfus). Elaine is complicated, difficult, and smart (with an IQ of 145). She's not dying to get married and have children, nor is she a career vixen. Instead, she's whiny and neurotic, but no more (and at times less) than the three guys with whom she spends her time. In all respects she is their equal and has no trouble pushing them around—literally, with her famous "get out" shove.

Unlike Ally and Ronnie (and most female sit-com stars), Elaine doesn't have a best girlfriend. Nor does she have even a single maternal instinct. She qualifies as an almost-brave dame because, although she is totally self-involved, she stands up for that silly self with wit and energy.

Men and women partners have long been a staple of detective fiction. Nora Charles, partner of her husband, Nick, in Dashiell Hammett's *The Thin Man*, is often so fluff-brained and drunk to distraction that she cannot be considered a brave dame. But S. J. Rozan's nineties hero, Lydia Chin, is. Born and raised in New York's Chinatown, Chin and her sometime partner Bill Smith are in the brave-dame-and-a-guy tradition extending from

A. A. Fair's Bertha Cool and Donald Lam (Fair is a pseudonym of Erle Stanley Gardner) and Frances Lockridge and Richard Lockridge's Pam and Jerry North.

These days, movies and TV are partnering up also for more serious sleuthing. Sometimes the man and woman can even contain themselves and not flirt, as with Mulder and Scully on *The X-Files*. (Personally, I detest that show, with its deadpan cool—a reprise of the Martin Landau/ Barbara Bain partnership on the old *Mission Impossible* series—and its subanthropodial conspiracy paranoia.) Far more appealing serious partners are Darby Shaw (Julia Roberts) and Gray Grantham (Denzel Washington) in *The Pelican Brief* (1993); these two are fine allies without the high-school sexual humidity of *The X-Files*.

You'd think that action movies would be perfect for displays of brave-dameship. Disappointingly, when women become main characters in action movies, they are often lacking in stature and self-assertion. Or clothes, as with Sharon Stone in *The Specialist* (1994)—naked or barely dressed here for a good part of the film—and Jean-Paul Gaultiered Milla Jovovich as Leeloo in *The Fifth Element* (1997).

Although there's plenty of action in *Speed*

(1994), Sandra Bullock's character, Annie, sits for most of the film (in the bus driver's seat) taking orders from Jack (Keanu Reeves). When finally she is allowed to get up, she ends up with explosives strapped to her chest. Her first remark when Jack finds her? "I'm sorry." And once he gets her out of that particular pickle, she manages to get herself handcuffed to a runaway subway train so that she (1) again can't go anywhere and (2) has to be rescued by Jack once more.

In *Speed 2: Cruise Control* (1997) she's not any better. As with the previous installment, the real hero here is the guy (Alex, played by Jason Patric). He's the one who gets to face down the evil cruise-ship hijacker Geiger (Willem Dafoe) while Annie shepherds people to lifeboats. While she doesn't qualify as a wimpette, Annie lacks the leadership qualities—decisiveness, authority—of a brave dame. The irony is that Bullock is an actress who exudes stamina and strength, and she's a natural for any action hero role. Too bad she can't always get the action.

Unlike Sandra Bullock, Helen Hunt doesn't look as if she could single-handedly hold off a natural disaster, but she does have a fine, strong presence; she's the picture of decency. As Jo Harding in *Twister* (1996), she does a little better than her colleague did in *Speed*. Jo leads a team of people who chase tornadoes for a living, and she gets to participate in the action—running, driving, and waiting out the winds in cramped spaces with the rest of the crew. And she spews more tornado talk than any of them.

Of course, Jo does all of this in a tight white tank top, with her long blond hair catching those twister winds just so, as if she never heard of the invention of the braid. And she spends a good part of the movie hung up on her colleague Bill. At the end of the film, when she winds up making out with him, I had the sense that this was really what all the tornado brouhaha was about. That dimmed Jo's glow for me.

Luckily, some notable female characters paired up with men in action flicks get to hold their own with those men physically, indulge in some badinage, and avoid stereotypical behavior. Alas, they still tend to be girlfriends or sidekicks to male main characters. However, these action dames are there for the action. They don't meander into it like Annie in *Speed*.

In *Lethal Weapon 3* (1992), Sergeant Lorna Cole (Rene Russo) is strong, smart, sexy, and funny and gets almost as much thrills and spills as the guy buddies Riggs (Mel Gibson) and Murtaugh (Danny Glover). While they bicker, she's incredibly cool. In the film's several shoot-'em-up sequences, she's a fierce fighter, kickboxing her way through various opponents. And she more than holds her own verbally in her one-on-one encounters with Riggs. She also has at least as many battle scars as he does, as she reveals when they compare them. The film could easily lose its PMS joke and lines like "Now, that's not a nice thing to say to a lady." It also would rank higher with me if Lorna hadn't been the only one of the three to get hit at the end and wind up limp as a lox, with Riggs as her protector. (In *Lethal Weapon 4*, Lorna gets pregnant with Riggs's baby and avers—while on the gurney on her way to the delivery room—that there isn't going to be a baby unless he marries her. Cute and ineffectual, a typical wimpette threat.)

Wai Lin, played by Michelle Yeoh, a Chinese spy in *Tomorrow Never Dies* (1997), appears to have taken karate lessons from the same trainer as Sergeant Lorna Cole. Like Lorna, she is a powerful fighter, leaving a string of corpses in her wake. She's also like Lorna in that she's an intelligent, independent, gorgeous babe who has a love scene with an equally good-looking male adversary—James Bond—who becomes an ally. Sad to say, Bond does have to save her at the end.

I have always needed my heroes to be good;

the antihero has my head but not my heart. So while I admire the boldness of *La Femme Nikita*, the moral compass of the main character spins too fast for me to consider her a brave dame. Still, she is one tough action hero. There have been two movies (a 1990 French version with Anne Parillaud and a 1993 American film called *Point of No Return* with Bridget Fonda). And now there's a USA Network television show (with Peta Wilson) based on the story of *La Femme Nikita*.

Nikita (called Maggie in *The Point of No Return*) starts out as a drug addict living on the streets in both the television show and the films. In the films, she kills a cop and is sentenced to death; on the television show, she is sentenced to life in prison for a murder she did not commit. In all three, the government fakes her death, and she wakes up in a top-secret agency that trains her as a combination spy, antiterrorist operative, and assassin. (The TV show plays down the hit-man angle.) Nikita's choice—which really isn't one—is to comply or face death.

She excels at her new work. She never blows her cover and, in the films, successfully pulls off several dangerous jobs on short notice. She falls in love, but she doesn't end up with a man. Rather, she uses the fact that her boss is in love with her to escape her fate as an assassin and start a new life alone. What is appealing about Nikita is that—unlike Wai Lin and Lorna Cole—she's no supporting player. The films and series are very much about her adventures and not about the men around her.

MANY OF THE SUCCESSFUL PROFESSIONAL women in film (both single and married) who manage not to be one-dimensional harridans or postfeminist basket cases have careers in politics. This category includes Libby Holden (Kathy Bates) in *Primary Colors,* Glenn Close in *Air Force One,* M (Judi Dench) in *Tomorrow Never Dies,* and Julia (Geena Davis) in *Speechless.* Of course, all of these women have secondary or behind-the-scenes jobs, and Libby Holden cannot take the heat; she commits suicide. Also, with the exception of Geena Davis's Julia, none is a main character.

Other competent working women who aren't too brittle or too simpering—and who are also actually seen at work, usually in traditionally male occupations—include the police officers played by Holly Hunter in *Copycat* (1995) and Laurie Metcalf in *Internal Affairs* (1990), forensic psychiatrist Molly Arrington (Frances McDormand, who seems to be competence personified) in *Primal Fear* (1996), and lawyer Gareth Peirce (Emma Thompson) in *In the Name of the Father* (1993). These women are smart, energetic, courageous, and passionate about their work. They're also decent people who turn the career-crone stereotype on its head. Unfortunately, as with the politicos, these are supporting roles, so I suppose I would call them supporting brave dames.

BRAVE DAMES

There are more brave dames in this chapter than any other. I think it reflects a recognition that women on their own, free of the burdens of catching a husband and being a madonna, have time to look at themselves and, instead of finding manacles, discover Wonder Woman wristlets. All right, so forget the superhuman accessories. But they at least have nothing holding them back from being their best.

Although the lovely, saintly Maria (Brigitte Helm) in Fritz Lang's silent film *Metropolis* (1926) worked to quell a revolt by slave laborers to ease their suffering, two more recent movies have featured brave dames who fight to rouse their fellow workers. In *Norma Rae* (1979) Sally Field is the eponymous hero who brings heart, soul, and head into organizing her fellow workers at a Southern textile mill. In *Silkwood* (1983) Meryl Streep plays Karen Silkwood, a worker at the Kerr-McGee nuclear plant in Oklahoma determined to help the people she works with by showing evidence of the company's negligence to a *New York Times* reporter and, through him, to the world. In the end, it costs her peace of mind, her lover, and her life, but for Silkwood there is no turning back.

In the film version of John Grisham's novel *The Pelican Brief* (1993), Julia Roberts is Darby Shaw, a law student sleeping with her law professor. Okay, not an auspicious start, but he is soon blown to bits. Intent on solving the murders of two Supreme Court justices, Darby writes a brief with a theory as to whodunit that ends up in the wrong hands—and puts her on the run for the rest of the film.

While she is being hunted she has plenty of opportunity to look like a frightened wimpette—which she does well. But she's not. She takes control by enlisting first a fellow student and then a Washington reporter (Denzel Washington) to help her hide and expose the culprits. Darby and the reporter work together, but she always holds the cards.

Perhaps even more surprising than the appealing

but fragile-seeming Julia Roberts in a brave dame role is Demi Moore, but she plays an excellent character, buzz-cut-sporting Navy SEAL trainee Jordan O'Neil, in *G.I. Jane* (1997). Jordan passionately wants to be the first female SEAL, not only to prove to herself she can do it, but also because, as she tells her boyfriend at the beginning of the film, the military tells women they can't be SEALs or on a submarine because there aren't any bathrooms for women there.

Jordan is mentally and physically tough—stronger than many of the men around her. (She endures more physical hardship than any female character in any movie I can recall.) She longs to be treated just like the men, whether that treatment is fair or unfair. She lets her commander see her topless in the shower, as he does with the men. Moore plays the moment with such guts that it is not the least titillating. *G.I. Jane* is too simplistic to be a great movie, but Jordan herself is a great dame.

Jodie Foster has played two of my favorite brave dames in recent movies—Clarice Starling in *The Silence of the Lambs* and Ellie Arroway in *Contact*. Director Jonathan Demme's 1991 film *The Silence of the Lambs*—and the Thomas Harris novel from which it's adapted—provides an exceptional female character in Clarice Starling. We know we're in for something different right from the first scene of the film, where Clarice is seen running and climbing as part of a grueling workout: She's got physical strength, and she won't quit. Shortly thereafter we learn that she's also intelligent, professional, independent, brave, kind, honest, and moral despite her youth and novice status.

Clarice is an FBI trainee who was orphaned at ten (her mother died even earlier) and is but "one generation up from white trash." She's assigned to interview the frightening serial killer Hannibal Lecter ("Hannibal the Cannibal," played by Anthony Hopkins) at his jail cell. Her mission is to use him to help get information about Buffalo Bill, another serial killer at large.

During her first visit to Lecter, his lecherous psychiatrist comes on to her, but she deals with him like a pro. Lecter himself is alternately useful and cruelly perceptive, immediately pointing out her good bag and cheap shoes and forcing her to repeat the obscenities uttered at her by his neighbor. Later he gets her to reveal one of the worst moments of her childhood. But Lecter's not just manipulating Clarice. It's a quid pro quo relationship, and she ends up getting information from Lecter that leads to the capture of Buffalo Bill.

Clarice reveals her smarts and her mental and physical toughness at other moments during the film. She picks up on Lecter's arcane clues and references. She orders a room full of unfriendly male officers out the door. She also deals with all varieties of gruesomeness. When faced with examining a victim's mutilated corpse that even the veterans can barely stand to smell or look at, she not only manages to dictate detailed notes but also is the only one to notice a cocoon in the throat, providing a crucial clue to Buffalo Bill. Clarice copes with all of this without flinching.

In a refreshing departure, Clarice doesn't have a love interest. She is truly on her own, with a female friend as her only confidante. But she doesn't give the impression that she's incapable of love; rather, it's just that she still has plenty of time for that. This film also deserves credit for its smart awareness of sexual harassment issues. Clarice is involved in several unpleasant incidents and, brave and diplomatic dame that she is, handles all with aplomb.

Jodie Foster has another great role (though no match for the noble Clarice) as astronomer Dr. Ellie Arroway in *Contact* (1997). Ellie is bright, brave, motivated, dedicated, and passionate about her calling since the age of eight. She is willing to fight and to go to any length to prove her belief that there is life beyond Earth.

Like Clarice, Ellie is alone in the world. She is

also alone in her work—no one believes in what she's doing until she gets a message from a distant galaxy that the whole world can see with her. By the end of the movie, after she's gone to that galaxy but can't prove she's been there, no one appears to believe her anymore. It turns out that the government is withholding information that supports her argument. Even though the whole world may doubt her, at no time is she portrayed as crazy or stupid.

Ellie never compromises her values. When she's interviewed for a seat on an interstellar flight, she is asked about her belief in God. She is an atheist, and though she knows it will lose her the seat, she refuses to lie or back down from her position. Later—after she has been to the galaxy and found faith—she refuses to lie about that.

Sandra Bullock's brave dame Angela Bennett in the thriller *The Net* (1995) (also a USA Network television series) isn't perfect. Her personal life is unusual at best, and she's another hunted victim, reacting to a situation she's thrown into. But she's passionate about something besides a man or kids. Yes, it's her computer, and okay, she lives a hermitlike life sitting in front of it, even ordering her pizza dinner via the Web. Her neighbors don't know her, even though she's lived in the same place for four years. Her only in-person contact with the outside world appears to be during visits to her mother, who has Alzheimer's—a particularly affecting subplot for an action film, showing not only Angela's loneliness, but her decency.

Angela makes a living doing something she loves—fixing computer problems. And when she's not working, she engages in plenty of cyberchat. She also goes on vacation to Cozumel by herself (bravery of a different sort), where she is seduced by the enemy—though she does point out she's not normally that kind of girl.

Once she inadvertently comes into possession of a disk that can control the world, Angela is on the run, and very much out of the house—since when she returns from vacation, the house has been emptied and is being sold. The evildoers steal her identity and create a new, criminal one for her, and no one believes she's Angela Bennett. She turns to the only person she can—a former lover who helps her for a while.

After he's out of the picture, Angela is truly on her own, fighting for her life—and to save the world from being controlled by cybercriminals. She's quick on her feet, clever, valiant, resourceful, and physically strong. She outruns the big bad guy on several occasions and slays him in the end, as well as overcoming great obstacles to save humanity by destroying the corrupt mainframe with a virus. Is this a brave dame or what?

ALLY AND RONNIE ASIDE, TELEVISION does provide competent, well-rounded, young, single professional women who qualify as brave dames. Examples from recent shows include criminal defense lawyers Lindsay Dole (Kelli Williams)—who, in one episode, demands equity in the firm—and Ellenor (Camryn Manheim) on *The Practice* (just how much these two, in their sensible shoes and wardrobes, differ from Ally McBeal was made clear when they appeared on a couple of "crossover" shows to work on the same case); assistant DA Claire Kincaid (Jill Hennessy) and psychiatrist Elizabeth Olivet (Carolyn McCormick) on *Law & Order*; detective Diane Russell (Kim Delaney) on *NYPD Blue*; detectives Kay Howard (Melissa Leo) and Laura Ballard (Callie Thorne), chief medical examiner Julianna Cox (Michelle Forbes), and Lieutenant Megan Russert (Isabella Hoffman) on *Homicide*; Detective Nina Moreno (Lauren Velez) on *New York Undercover*, who has lost her daughter and two husbands; Dr. Elizabeth Corday (Alex Kingston), Dr. Susan Lewis (Sherry Stringfield), nurse Carol Hathaway (Julianna Margulies), and physician assistant Jeanie Boulet

(Gloria Reuben) on *ER;* and Dr. Lisa Catera (Stacy Edwards) on *Chicago Hope*.[9] Unfortunately, they're all supporting brave dames.

Older single professional women are portrayed in a less flattering light. They're either terribly stern and hard-boiled, as with Helen Mirren's detective character on the British import *Prime Suspect* or Star Fleet captain Kathryn Janeway (Kate Mulgrew) on *Star Trek: Voyager,* or a bit too much the meddling old biddy, as with mystery writer and sleuth Jessica Fletcher (Angela Lansbury) on *Murder, She Wrote*. It's a subtle way of showing that smart, independent women wind up with the traits of the traditional old maid.

Goofy, funny, bighearted, and loaded with self-deprecating charm, Ellen DeGeneres of *Ellen*[10] seemed a worthy successor to Lucille Ball and Mary Tyler Moore. She was a single woman—a lesbian, it turned out—who could take care of herself. She bought a bookstore (which she later sold) and then a house. She was also a loyal friend.

9. For more on some of the women on the cop shows mentioned, see Ileane Rudolph, "Arresting Women," *TV Guide*, Mar. 28– Apr. 3, 1998, p. 18.
10. The media coverage of *Ally McBeal* may be eclipsed only by the coverage of Ellen (the actress and the character) coming out. One of the more notable pieces was Bruce Handy, "Roll Over, Ward Cleaver," *Time,* Apr. 14, 1997, p. 78.

But in the show's last season, Ellen became a lot less engaging. She was no longer an entrepreneur, jumping instead from one job to another, and spent too much time mooning over her new girlfriend. Nevertheless, this was also the only season in which she was out of the closet, and she gave the American public much-needed insight into what it means to be a lesbian. And that was a truly brave act.

Brave dames have now begun to spring up on previously male-dominated sci-fi TV shows. In addition to Captain Janeway, these characters include half-Borg, half-human babe Seven of Nine (Jeri Ryan) and chief engineer B'Elanna Torres (Roxann Dawson) on *Star Trek: Voyager,* and science officer Jadzia Dax (Terry Farrell) (who weds her Klingon boyfriend) and freedom fighter Kira Nerys (Nana Visitor) (who gives birth to a surrogate child) on the syndicated *Star Trek: Deep Space Nine.*[11]

Xena (Lucy Lawless) on *Xena: Warrior Princess* is another strong, tough, agile mythic mistress of the martial arts. Xena's backstory is that she starts out with an obsession to prove herself the ultimate

11. For more on these sci-fi women, see Dan Snierson, "Lust in Space," *Entertainment Weekly,* Sept. 19, 1997, p. 42; Michael Logan, "Solar Sisters," *TV Guide,* Nov. 8–14, 1997, p. 18.

warrior and sets out to kill Hercules in her quest for power. After she realizes she's lost sight of her own humanity, she experiences a conversion and becomes Hercules's ally and love interest. She then heads home to begin a new life helping the oppressed and needy and atoning for her past sins.

After defeating the barbaric Draco and saving her home village, Xena travels the ancient world with her best friend, Gabrielle (Renee O'Connor), to fight tyranny and injustice. Always on the move, Xena is the rare female character who doesn't even have a home and hearth to defend.

In fending off mythological monsters, barbaric tribes, slave traders, and a host of other evils along her way, Xena always tries to solve things peacefully. However, when necessary, she uses her physical strength and agility, wields a discuslike weapon called a chakram, and applies the "Xena touch," a two-fingered pinch on the pressure points of the neck.

My main problem with Xena is that the show is so campy, amateurish, and ineptly written that it's barely watchable. The good news is that once you get past the cheesy production values and wooden dialogue, Xena is one hell of a brave dame.

The last few years have seen a proliferation of teenage brave dames on TV who get to have adventures. Several have supernatural powers, including Buffy the Vampire Slayer (based on the 1992 film that starred Kristy Swanson); Sabrina, the Teenage Witch; and Alex Mack on Nickelodeon's *The Secret World of Alex Mack*, an awesome Frisbee player who is able to morph into invisible quicksilver. Other, more human brave dames include Moesha on the show of the same name, Clarissa on *Clarissa Explains It All*, and Shelby Woo on Nickelodeon's *The Mystery Files of Shelby Woo*, a high-school student and intern at the police department who ends up fighting crime herself. Finally there's the stylish animated lead of the MTV animated series *Daria,* who is sarcastic, pessimistic, sensible, brainy, quick-witted, and wise beyond her years,[12] as well as smart, determined young Lisa on *The Simpsons.*

All of these heroes have good sense and decent values, and all—even those with extraordinary powers—face the problems of normal girls.[13] Buffy the Vampire Slayer (Sarah Michelle Gellar) didn't choose her fate as the one girl in the world with the strength and skill to hunt down vampires. And she doesn't always enjoy defending humanity,

12. For a discussion of *Daria*, see Alex Kuczynski, "Beavis and Butt-head's Feminine Side," *The New York Times,* May 11, 1998, p. D10.
13. For an excellent discussion of teenage television heroines, see Ginia Bellafante, "Bewitching Teen Heroines," *Time,* May 5, 1997, p. 82.

often preferring to spend time with her boyfriend, Angel, or hang out at the local club, The Bronze, rather than spend sleepless nights keeping the undead in check.

But Buffy's reluctance never keeps her from doing her job as well as she can, even when it requires making sacrifices. She battles demons in every episode. When she's not using her physical power—kicking, punching, outrunning, or breaking the nose of an enemy—in order to off bloodsuckers and save the world, she's usually using her mental prowess to deflect an evil spell or investigate evil-doings. She routinely rescues her mother, her friends, and even her ungrateful nemesis Cordelia.

Buffy isn't invulnerable. She weeps and gets scared on occasion, but she almost always swallows her fear and saves the world. Her normal teenage problems include parents who have split up and a boyfriend who mistreats her after she loses her virginity with him. She's not in the popular crowd at her high school, and it's tough to get any homework done after pulling an all-nighter slaying monsters. But a brave dame's gotta do what she's gotta do.

Madeleine L'Engle's great children's novel *A Wrinkle in Time* is fantasy of a far different sort. In part science fiction, in part theological musing, it's a wonderfully accessible work for young readers. Its hero, Meg, sets off on a quest through space and time to seek her lost father. Her courage in facing the darkest forces of the cosmos and her own fears is not just exemplary; it's inspiring.

Likewise, E. B. White's exquisite tale of the beautiful, intelligent spider Charlotte and how she saves the dear pig Wilbur gives kids another brave dame to hold in their hearts. *Charlotte's Web* deserves its status as a classic; few people have the humanity of this singular spider.

Disney, too, has provided some memorable heroes for youngsters in its animated features over the last decade. The standouts are Mulan and Pocahontas. (Belle in *Beauty and the Beast* and Ariel in *The Little Mermaid* are too much the man-pleasers for my taste.)[14]

The title character in *Pocahontas* (1995) is truly a brave dame. She's independent, proud, strong, moral, fearless, and remarkable in that she chooses to stay with her people rather than follow her man at the end. It is a nice twist, because the film changes the Pocahontas legend and makes the protagonist more of a responsible leader of her people. (The actual woman married a settler, John Rolfe, and went with him to England.)

14. For a discussion of Belle, Ariel, and Pocahontas, see Caryn James, "Belle and Ariel Never Chose Duty over Love," *The New York Times,* June 18, 1995, Arts and Leisure section, p. 13.

The warrior Mulan in the 1998 film of the same name has many of the admirable traits as Pocahontas—she too is intrepid and strong. She's also an impressive fighter, passing herself off as a member of the all-male Chinese army for much of the movie.

Early in the film, when she has a disastrous meeting with a matchmaker, we learn that Mulan isn't cut out for an arranged marriage. When her father is then conscripted to fight the Huns, Mulan, realizing he's too weak to survive battle, chops off her hair, dons his armor, and rides her horse to the army camp.

Mulan lights cannons, survives an avalanche on horseback, and—like her predecessor Pocahontas—saves a man's life. Even after she's discovered, Mulan provides crucial information to the Chinese army, then takes on and defeats the leader of the Huns. In an unprecedented act, the Chinese emperor bows to Mulan, who has saved his empire. And, like that other brave dame Jane Eyre, she gets the guy.

It's a giant leap from the wonderful, market-tested world of Disney to the more idiosyncratic world of adult fiction, but a leap worth making, because there are more brave dames per capita on the page than on the screen. I don't know why this is so, although I suspect that the collaborative art and commerce of movies and television—unless controlled by the sensibility of a powerful director or star—reflects more of an establishment vision of our culture: conservative, male-dominated, more responsive to popular prejudices and communal desires. The novel, usually the work of a single person, can be as nonconformist as the author wishes: There are no story meetings, no recruited audience screenings, no advertisers to placate. Further, instead of the camera's investigation of the perceivable, we have the narrator's exploration of the psychological. The reader does not merely rely on dialogue and visual clues to discern a character's emotional state, but is often privy to the character's thoughts.

From Agatha Christie's three female sleuths—Miss Marple, Ariadne Oliver, and Tuppence Beresford—on, some of the bravest dames in fiction have been seeking to discover whodunit. No matter how flawed the detective, they all have a single-minded need to track down the culprit (almost always a murderer) and see that the scales of justice, out of whack because a life has been taken, come back into balance. From hard-boiled private investigators like Sara Paretsky's V. I. Warshawski to more establishment types like P. D. James's police detective Cordelia Gray, Linda Fairstein's assistant district attorney Alexandra Cooper, and

Amanda Cross's Professor Kate Fansler, the women detectives in whodunits have a keen moral code and a willingness to follow the clues to the truth, no matter how fearsome the journey.

The marvel of it is that there are now so many brave dames in detective fiction, a list of them all would turn into a catalog. Just a few of my favorites: Sue Grafton's northern California PI Kinsey Milhone, Nevada Barr's National Park Service ranger Anna Pigeon, Sparkle Hayter's reporter Robin Hudson, Lisa Scottoline's Philadelphia lawyers Benedetta "Bennie" Rosato and Grace Rossi, and Valerie Wilson Wesley's Newark, New Jersey, PI Tamara Hayle. Each year of this decade has brought another shelf's worth of women who are more interested in seeking justice than a husband.

Until recently, some of the few brave dames in contemporary fiction were to be found in what have been called the "glitzy" novels of Sidney Sheldon, Judith Krantz, and Jackie Collins. While it is true that their protagonists are all gorgeous, with breasts pointing north, these women are almost always out of the house and doing work they love. They each have a passion that has nothing to do with their being women and everything to do with their being bright, industrious individuals.

Maybe it takes time to get our cultural bearings after a revolution, but I sense that some psychological and social breakthroughs are finally making their way into fiction. It is not that we have become a nation of superwomen, but that a more realistic view of who we are is starting to take hold, driving out some of the wimpettes, bringing in new heroes.

Rachel, the eldest of seven in a Hasidic family, understands that her passionate heart and inquiring mind are not an asset in the controlled, tradition-bound world into which she has been born. Pearl Abraham's *The Romance Reader* tells the story of an unlikely brave dame who must choose between faith and family, on one hand, and her own independent spirit, on the other.

Eleanor Lipman's *The Inn at Lake Devine* (1998) seems at first almost a romp. In the early sixties, in response to an inquiry about rooms in a Vermont inn, Natalie Marx's parents receive a letter that ends: "Our guests who feel most comfortable here, and return year after year, are Gentiles." Indeed, the story of Natalie's nonviolent but nonetheless formidable assault on the no-Jews-allowed hotel is a witty, spirited social comedy. But the narrative of Natalie's hurt and outrage at being left out of America, her determination to right those wrongs, and her growing willingness to accept the complexity of justice and love is nothing short of heroic.

Imagine George Orwell and Terry Gilliam collaborating on a brave dame. Or Ray Bradbury and Sojourner Truth working together to give us an American hero. Colson Whitehead's *The Intuitionist* (1998) is an enormously accomplished first novel, a meditation on race and technology and imagination that is absolutely dazzling. Dazzling too is his hero, Lila Mae Watson, an elevator inspector. An elevator inspector? Yes. Lila Mae lives in an alternative America where she is—in the book's language—her city's first colored elevator inspector, and the most accurate. She is one of the Intuitionists and can tell merely by closing her eyes and concentrating just what is going on in the machinery. But the Intuitionists are under attack by more conservative elements, and an elevator she has just inspected suddenly goes into free fall. How did it happen? Sabotage? Is there a power greater than the Intuitionists'? Could she possibly have made a dreadful mistake? First by chance, then by design, Lila Mae becomes the seeker of truth and the righter of wrongs. She faces public and private disgrace, threats from the pols, kidnapping by the mob, and terrible loneliness with the steadfast commitment of the truly just. How great it would be if there were more like her in life; how wonderful that we have such a brave dame in art.

6

Some Conclusions, and Some Brave Dames You Might Like to Get to Know

SAMUEL GOLDWYN IS REPUTED TO have said, "If you want to send a message, call Western Union." Propaganda rarely makes good art. And while hewing to a politically correct line will avoid giving offense, good art—original, vigorous, iconoclastic—often is offensive. But whether we label them messages or not, novels and movies and TV shows do communicate, and the meaning is often clear: Wimpettes live happily ever after. Brave dames go bonkers or go it alone or go to hell in a handbasket.

Clearly, there is no conspiracy of writers, actors, directors, and studio and network executives scheming to keep females in their place by slipping subliminal messages into books, TV, and movies. If asked whether they think women are the equals of men, most of them would say yes. Still, cultural prejudice against independent women is so powerful that it cannot be overcome in a few decades, even by women themselves.

I have called myself a feminist for over thirty years now, yet I recall how enchanted I was when Prince Richard Gere came to save Cinderella first from a life of whoredom, then one of poverty in *Pretty Woman*—and enchanted also when he carried his other Cinderella away from her drab factory job in *An Officer and a Gentleman*. My first reaction to the angel women paying back the devil men in spades in Olivia Goldsmith's lively novel *The First Wives Club* was "Hot damn!" What pleases me may also disappoint me or even anger me.

The classic ending for a comedy is a marriage. I was taught to view the lack of one—a woman going it alone—as a tragedy. Too bad. But look on the bright side. Cinderella and her wimpette sisters may still be insinuating their teeny feet forward and tippytoeing into my psyche, but the characters who have truly lived for me are the brave dames, because they genuinely *lived*. No one breathed for them, no one told them what or how to think. So here are some of my favorite works that feature them. Are all my recommendations great art? No. Are they superior to works featuring wimpettes? Sometimes, although no one with half a brain would say *Buffy the Vampire Slayer* has greater aesthetic merit than *Anna Karenina*.

Anyway, here are the women and girls (and one spider) I love. I wish you the pleasure of their company.

MOVIES

Adam's Rib
Alice Doesn't Live Here Anymore
All About Eve
Auntie Mame
Broadcast News
Buffy the Vampire Slayer
Clueless
Fargo
Friendly Persuasion
G.I. Jane
His Girl Friday
Norma Rae
Silkwood
Terminator 2
The Color Purple
The Silence of the Lambs
The Wizard of Oz

NOVELS

A Handmaid's Tale (Margaret Atwood)
An Unsuitable Job for a Woman (P. D. James)
I Capture the Castle (Dodie Smith)
Jane Eyre (Charlotte Brontë)
My Antonia (Willa Cather)
Pride and Prejudice (Jane Austen)
Smilla's Sense of Snow (Peter Høeg)
The Inn at Lake Devine (Eleanor Lipman)
The Silence of the Lambs (Thomas Harris)
The Intuitionist (Colson Whitehead)
The Romance Reader (Pearl Abraham)

FOR CHILDREN AND ADULTS:

A Wrinkle in Time (Madeleine L'Engle)
Charlotte's Web (E. B. White)

And the brave dame detective novels of the following authors:

Linda Barnes, Nevada Barr, Amanda Cross, Linda Fairstein, Elizabeth George, Sue Grafton, Sparkle Hayter, Laura Lippman, Sara Paretsky, Elizabeth Peters, Lisa Scottoline, and Valerie Wilson Wesley.

TELEVISION

Alice
Buffy the Vampire Slayer
Cagney & Lacey
Dr. Quinn, Medicine Woman
Murphy Brown
The Mary Tyler Moore Show
The Big Valley
The Simpsons
Xena: Warrior Princess

Index

ABOUT THE AUTHOR

SUSAN ISAACS would have liked "to have come into this world in a thatched cottage in the Cotswolds," but was, in fact, born in Brooklyn in 1943. She attended Queens College, where she majored in English and economics, and then worked at *Seventeen* magazine, where she rose from editorial assistant, writing advice to the lovelorn, to senior editor. In 1968, Isaacs married Elkan Abramowitz, a trial lawyer. They have two children, Andrew and Elizabeth.

Isaacs is the #1 bestselling author of *Compromising Positions, Close Relations, Almost Paradise, Shining Through, Magic Hour, After All These Years, Lily White,* and *Red, White and Blue.*

She made her debut as a screenwriter with the

film version of *Compromising Positions,* which starred Susan Sarandon and Raul Julia. Isaacs wrote and coproduced her second film, *Hello Again,* in 1987. Shelley Long, Judith Ivey, and Corbin Bernsen headed the cast. The film adaptation of *Shining Through* was released in 1991 and featured Melanie Griffith, Michael Douglas, Liam Neeson, and John Gielgud.

Isaacs is a member of the National Book Critics Circle and the International Association of Crime Writers. She is on the national board of Mystery Writers of America and is chair of its Committee on Free Expression. She is also a member of the executive committee of PEN.

A Note on The Library of Contemporary Thought

This exciting new monthly series tackles today's most provocative, fascinating, and relevant issues, giving top opinion makers a forum to explore topics that matter urgently to themselves and their readers. Some will be think pieces. Some will be research oriented. Some will be journalistic in nature. The form is wide open, but the aim is the same: to say things that need saying.

Now available from
THE LIBRARY OF CONTEMPORARY THOUGHT

VINCENT BUGLIOSI
NO ISLAND OF SANITY
Paula Jones v. Bill Clinton
The Supreme Court
on Trial

JOHN FEINSTEIN
THE FIRST COMING
Tiger Woods:
Master or Martyr?

PETE HAMILL
NEWS IS A VERB
Journalism at the End of the
Twentieth Century

CARL HIAASEN
TEAM RODENT
How Disney Devours
the World

SEYMOUR M. HERSH
AGAINST ALL ENEMIES
Gulf War Syndrome: The
War Between America's
Ailing Veterans and Their
Government

**EDWIN
SCHLOSSBERG**
INTERACTIVE
EXCELLENCE
Defining and Developing
New Standards for the
Twenty-first Century

ANNA QUINDLEN
HOW READING
CHANGED MY LIFE

**WILLIAM STERLING
AND STEPHEN WAITE**
BOOMERNOMICS
Technology, Globalization,
and the Future of Your
Money in the Upcoming
Generational Warfare

JIMMY CARTER
THE VIRTUES OF
AGING

Coming from

THE LIBRARY OF CONTEMPORARY THOUGHT

*America's most original writers
give you a piece of their minds*

Harry Shearer
Stephen Jay Gould
Robert Hughes
Jonathan Kellerman
Joe Klein
Walter Mosley
Donna Tartt
Don Imus
Nora Ephron

**Look for these titles coming soon from
The Library of Contemporary Thought**

HARRY SHEARER
IT'S THE STUPIDITY, STUPID
Why (Some) People Hate Clinton and Why
the Rest of Us Have to Watch

STEPHEN JAY GOULD
ROCKS OF AGES
Science and Religion in the Fullness of Life